The Little Book of

TIBETAN RITES AND RITUALS

The Little Book of
TIBETAN RITES
AND RITUALS

Simple Practices for Rejuvenating
the Mind, Body, and Spirit

JUDY TSUEI

Published by:
Ulysses Press
PO Box 3440
Berkeley, CA 94703
www.ulyssespress.com

ISBN: 978-1-64604-252-4
Library of Congress Control Number: 2021937756

Printed in the United States by Versa Press
10 9 8 7 6 5 4 3 2 1

Acquisitions editor: Claire Sielaff
Managing editor: Claire Chun
Project editor: Bridget Thoreson
Editor: Phyllis Elving
Proofreader: Michele Anderson
Front cover design: Rebecca Lown
Interior design and layout: what!design @ whatweb.com
Production: Jake Flaherty, Yesenia Garcia-Lopez
Artwork: exercises pages 60, 64, 67, 69, 72, 72 ji_production/fiverr; page 12 © Natali Li -TibetMeds/shutterstock.com

For my po po, Ai-Nan Tsuei.
Thank you for always being in my life, wherever you are now.

CONTENTS

Chapter 1

AN INTRODUCTION TO TIBETAN BUDDHISM

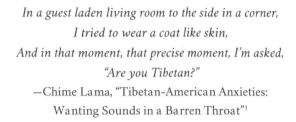

In a guest laden living room to the side in a corner,
I tried to wear a coat like skin,
And in that moment, that precise moment, I'm asked,
"Are you Tibetan?"
—Chime Lama, "Tibetan-American Anxieties:
Wanting Sounds in a Barren Throat"[1]

YOU ARE MORE POWERFUL THAN YOU KNOW

Approximately 13.8 billion years ago, the universe began with what's known as the Big Bang. The atoms created by that event would integrate into everything that exists today, big or small, including the human body. That means that within us are oxygen, carbon, hydrogen, nitrogen, calcium, phosphorus, potassium, sulfur, sodium, chlorine, and magnesium—all of which came from a process called "galactic chemical evolution."[2]

Many of the elements in our bodies were formed in stars over the course of billions of years and multiple star lifetimes—we're made of this "star stuff," yet in our modern world, it can be easy to forget how magical we truly are. Thankfully, we can draw upon ancient mindfulness traditions to create a sense of being grounded and to remind ourselves, as we adapt to an ever-evolving world, that we are indeed as powerful and expansive as the universe. One of these ancient traditions is a series of Five Tibetan Rites first brought to public awareness in a 1939 book by Peter Kelder titled *The Eye of Revelation*.

Kelder tells the story of a British explorer—Colonel Bradford—who had spent years searching for a secret paradise in the Himalayas. Bradford had heard that Tibetan lamas, considered spiritual teachers in Tibetan Buddhism, maintained an unparalleled sense of health and vitality. However, there's not a lot you can find about who author Kelder is. Some believe it's a pseudonym, which then also calls into question who Bradford was and whether he really existed. (More about this from expert Carolinda Witt later in this chapter.) On Penguin Random House's website under "About the Author" it says, "Well versed in the Tibetan Rites of Rejuvenation since the 1930s, Peter Kelder is alive and well, living in California. He is the author of *Ancient Secrets of the Fountain of Youth*." You'll learn more on what we know about Kelder throughout this book.

While similar to yoga rituals that originated in India, the Five Tibetan Rites are notably different in that they're dubbed "The

Fountain of Youth." This isn't the mythical spring that restores the youth of anyone who drinks or bathes in its waters, mistakenly linked to Spanish explorer Ponce de León and now a tourist attraction in St. Augustine, Florida.[3] Instead, these Five Tibetan Rites—which Bradford purportedly learned from lamas in a hidden monastery in Tibet—are a simple exercise system thought to bring health and rejuvenation.

This book will introduce the Five Tibetan Rites as they've been popularly taught, including modifications adapting them to a modern lifestyle, and will offer an overview of selected traditional Tibetan philosophies, beliefs, and practices. Please note that because *your* body, *your* being, and *your* life are unique, your own experience with these Rites and rituals may vary from that of others.

Most importantly, every effort has been made to be respectful of Tibetan traditions in order to honor a beautiful culture that has gone through tremendous challenges and injustices.

The Tibetan National Anthem states the following:

> *By the spread of Buddha's teachings in the ten directions,*
> *may everyone throughout the world*
> *enjoy the glories of happiness and peace.*

May the pages that follow offer you a pathway in one of those directions.

DISCOVERY OF THE FIVE TIBETAN RITES

To date, versions of Kelder's book have been translated into more than a dozen languages and have sold millions of copies. In several of these, you'll find pages of testimonials from individuals of all ages around the world attesting to how the Rites have healed ailments, renewed vitality, and harmonized invisible energy within the body. In 1985, the original book was expanded and updated with an edition titled *Ancient Secret of the Fountain of Youth*, featuring a "Lost Chapter."

In this newer edition, Kelder recounts how he became the keeper of this ancient wisdom in that he was seated in a California park reading the afternoon paper when an elderly gentleman ("Colonel Bradford, as I shall call him—though it is not his real name") came to sit beside him. Appearing to be in his late 60s, gray and balding, Bradford revealed that he was a retired British Army officer who had also served in the diplomatic corps for the Crown and was therefore well traveled.

Kelder shares that Bradford had heard a tale of a group of lamas, or Tibetan clerics, who, cut off from the world by expansive mountain ranges, had discovered the secrets of eternal youth and passed the knowledge down for thousands of years.[4]

Though Bradford asked Kelder to accompany him to find the lamas, Kelder demurred. Years later, after moving on with his life, Kelder received a letter from Bradford, who claimed to be close to finding what he was looking for. Months passed again, and another letter arrived. Then one day, Kelder heard from his doorman that a Bradford was there to see him. Throwing open his door, he was shocked to find a tall, young individual with thick, dark hair. "Weren't you expecting me?" Bradford asked. He shared with Kelder that he had found the lamas, who welcomed him. Though they initially called him "The Ancient One," his transformation soon became so noticeable that it was no longer an accurate moniker.

Since the publication of Kelder's book in 1939, there have been skeptics who've said that the Five Tibetan Rites, supposedly more than 2,500 years old, are not actually authentic to Tibet. Some question the myriad health-benefit claims and whether Bradford actually existed, since little is known of Kelder. Experts have noted that a similarity exists between the Five Tibetan Rites and authentic Tibetan 'phrul 'khor yoga exercises. Proponents assert that the Rites are a genuine form of *Yantra yoga*—one of the oldest recorded systems of yoga in the world, originally taken from an authentic Indo-Tibetan tantric lineage.

While modern culture has viewed tantra with a lens heavily focused on sex, it is actually an ancient Indian religious movement focused on the path toward enlightenment, one that seeks to harness a wide variety of experiences and energies in order to do so. Tantra practitioners believe that being guided by a teacher in esoteric practices—such as *mantra* (sacred words and phrases), *mudra* (ritualized sacred hand gestures), *mandalas* (diagrams of the universe)—can help you achieve "awakening" within just one lifetime. Tantra literally means "thread" or "loom"; you are weaving together the strands of the sutras or basic forms of Buddhist scriptures. [5]

THE CONTROVERSY OVER THE FIVE TIBETAN RITES, BY CAROLINDA WITT

Carolinda Witt has taught the Five Tibetan Rites to more than 45,000 people around the world over the past 21 years. Her method of learning the Rites is called T5T and incorporates natural, full breathing. The following is her take on both the controversy surrounding the origin of the Rites and their benefits.

I am often asked if the Five Tibetan Rites are real or if someone has made them up. Despite having carried out a vast amount of research, I have been unable to find a definitive source to prove their authenticity, age, or origins.

Twenty-one years ago, I read the original 1939 book, *The Eye of Revelation,* and was totally entranced. I wanted to share them with others and have never tired of hearing people describe the great benefits they have received. But, it was my own experience of practicing the Rites that convinced me they worked—and I have not shifted from this viewpoint to this day. For me, this is proof that the Rites are authentic.

However, let's dig into the past a bit:

The Eye of Revelation publishers claim the Rites are "25 centuries" (479 BC) old. This places them during the lifetime of Buddha (around the 5th to 4th century BC), who traveled throughout the fertile Indus-Ganga Plains teaching meditation practices and guidelines for attaining enlightenment—in other words, yoga practices as we understand them today: the cross-legged posture (*asana*) for meditation, contemplation of the breath (*pranayama*), meditation (*dhyana*), withdrawal of the senses (*pratyahara*), and the ethical guidelines (restraints and observances) of the *yamas* and *niyamas* with the goal of attaining *samadhi* (bliss).

I am not an expert on Tibetan Buddhism, but in broad terms, Tibetan Buddhism evolved from the later stages of Indian Buddhism and incorporated various indigenous Tibetan practices. Bön, the pre-Buddhist religion of Tibet, is similar to Tibetan Buddhism, although technical terms and viewpoints are explained differently. Controversy about which religion influenced the other remains uncertain, but what is unique to early Bön is a strong belief in the afterlife, particularly the in-between state and the use of animal sacrifice.[6]

Records from this period are scarce but well documented, and there is no mention of the Rites. The primary method of sharing knowledge was oral—traditionally passed from master to student, which means we have little chance of discovering the Rites' elusive history. This is further compounded by the Chinese Communist regime's invasion of Tibet in 1950, when they ransacked and destroyed 97 percent of Tibet's monasteries. Sadly, so many ancient religious texts have been lost forever.[7]

Perhaps the source of the Rites is more recent?

From the scans of a rare copy of the 1939 *Eye of Revelation* and the equally rare 1946 updated edition—I have literally picked both versions apart, looking for clues. I took into account four perspectives: the publisher's, the author's, the story as told by the protagonist, and the lamas' teachings as relayed by the protagonist, Colonel Bradford.

Let's start with the author, Peter Kelder.

Is this his real name, or is it made up? So far, the only thing we know about Kelder is that he registered the copyright for his 1939 and 1946 versions of his book and that his publisher was based in Burbank, California. Some people believe Peter Kelder was a pseudonym for James Hilton, the author of *Lost Horizon*, which was published in 1933 and made into a film by Frank Capra in 1937. Hilton's book is best remembered as the origin of Shangri-La, a fictional utopian lamasery located high in the mountains of Tibet. But why would Hilton need to write a second book linked to his fictional account in someone else's name? Why not simply use his own?

I believe the skepticism over Kelder's name is due to the story's protagonist using a pseudonym, Colonel Bradford. This and Bradford's incorrect statement that the dervishes spin clockwise, when in fact, they spin counter-clockwise. Bradford refers to the dervishes as the Mawlawiyah [sic], a 13th-century fraternity of Sufis (Muslim mystics) founded by the Persian Sufi poet Rūmī (d. 1273).[8] Could their spinning have been the inspiration for Rite No 1—The Spin—or is it from somewhere else entirely? If the Rites are from a later period than the publishers stated in *The Eye of Revelation*, then the search continues.

Are the benefits claimed for practicing the Rites real?

Some extraordinary claims have been made for practicing the Rites, and some of them are genuine. However, some highly exaggerated claims made by some unscrupulous internet marketers and a few people seeking to build a mystical reputation for themselves exist: "Throw your glasses away; your wrinkles will all disappear," and so on.

Unfortunately, this has tarnished the Rites' reputation, led to unrealistic expectations of improvements in health and physical appearance, and the inevitable disappointments. Written in the glowing language of the time, *The Eye of Revelation* has contributed to this skepticism by making statements like "even his hair, which had grown back, held no trace of gray." In all of my years of teaching, I have never seen people's hair turn dark again, and neither have any of my students reported it.

I believe this statement about hair darkening and the suggestion to rub fresh unsalted butter onto the scalp to make it grow is not part of the lamas' instructions to Bradford and was added by the publisher. Tibetan monks remove all the hair from their heads and are intentionally bald.

Yes, there *are* genuine benefits from practicing the Rites, a list of which appears on my website.[9] Benefits include an increase in energy, strength, flexibility, vitality, mental clarity, and well-being. I compiled these from students' workshop feedback forms and from people who have written in and shared their experiences. There are also some minor detox effects, also listed on my website, that people can experience temporarily. These include headaches, runny noses, slight nausea, initial fatigue, and so on. Most people view these as proof that the Rites are working.

To sum up: I believe the movements themselves produce similar benefits for most people. However, the degree to which they experience these benefits is very different. Some experience a great deal of change, others less so, and some don't notice much at all, except a 'knowing' or a feeling that the Rites are good for them. These benefits won't change even if we do find out where the Rites come from (or not).

Is it OK to modify the Rites to suit your individual needs?

The instructions on how to perform the Rites in *The Eye of Revelation* are minimal. That's part of their charm, but most beginners will require more in-depth instruction and perhaps modifications. We are much more sedentary than the monks who gave us the Rites, and the truth is, there is no one-size-fits-all body.

All movement, including the Rites, evolves over time as new research and experience find new and better ways of avoiding injury and enhancing performance. The Rites are repetitive movements, and a solid foundation in technique is essential.

If you need to bend your knees when doing the 2nd Rite or avoid leaning back as far in the 3rd Rite, or use a prop for your hands in the 4th and 5th Rites—go ahead and do it! You will still get the same benefits from the Rites as everyone else does.

> *Happy spinning, and remember to enjoy the journey as much as the destination.*
>
> *—Carolinda Witt*

Chapter 2

ABOUT TIBET, PAST TO PRESENT

Tashi delek.
—*Traditional Tibetan greeting meaning "Blessings and good luck" or "May all auspicious signs come to this environment"*

THE LANDSCAPE

The Great Wall of China, frequently billed as the only man-made object visible from space, actually isn't. "The only thing you can see from the Moon," according to Apollo 12 astronaut Alan Bean, "is a beautiful sphere, mostly white, some blue and patches of yellow, and every once in a while some green vegetation."[10]

What you *can* see when looking at satellite images of China is Tibet, the remote and mainly Buddhist territory known as the "roof of the world." At one million square miles, the Tibet area encompasses the entire Tibetan Plateau. This includes all the counties of the

"Tibet Autonomous Region" and 95 percent of Qinghai Province, plus southwest Gansu, northern Sichuan, western Sichuan, and far northwest Yunnan provinces—about one-quarter of China's landmass.

Under China's occupation, Tibet has been divided up, renamed, and incorporated, with little reference to the original borders between its provinces. When China refers to Tibet, it means the "Tibet Autonomous Region" or TAR, which includes only U-Tsang and part of Kham. The rest of Kham was divided between the Chinese provinces of Sichuan and Yunnan; Amdo was divided between Gansu, Sichuan, and Qinghai provinces.

Governed as an autonomous region of China, the Tibet Autonomous Region at 474,300 square miles makes up roughly half of the total Tibet area. The historic territory of Tibet, on the other hand, would make the world's 10th-largest nation by area. Its punishing terrain, high altitude, and hypoxic atmosphere have made Tibet one of the most sparsely populated areas of the planet, with fewer than six people per square mile. Throughout the remainder of this book, we will mainly be referencing the Tibet Autonomous Region when speaking of Tibet.

Tibetans share common ancestry with the Chinese, Japanese, Mongol, and Siberian populations and strongly resemble some Native Americans, but they have their own unique genetic variation that lets them thrive at high altitudes. Sometimes called a "superathlete" gene, this helps sherpas and other Tibetans breathe at altitudes above 13,000 feet, where the limited oxygen supply makes most people feel sick. Ann Gibbons, in *Science* magazine, noted that researchers found that while Andean highlanders have adapted to such thin air by adding *more* oxygen-carrying hemoglobin to their blood, Tibetans have adapted by having *less* hemoglobin. Scientists think this helps them avoid serious problems such as clots and strokes caused when the blood thickens with more hemoglobin-laden cells.[11]

Award-winning American journalist Barbara Demick explores this hidden corner of the world in her book *Eat the Buddha: Life and Death in a Tibetan Town.*

"In every direction, an expanse of nubby green carpet rises and falls with the contours of the mountains. The villages along the road consist of clusters of squat earthen houses. Shaggy yaks and sheep ignore the few passing cars. At key points along the road are offerings to the deities that Tibetans believe inhabit every mountain pass and hill. Prayer flags, sun-bleached to pale pastels, flutter from the mountain ridges."[12]

Hosting the highest mountains in the world, Tibet is a unique geological feature. Three Asian rivers—the Yangtze, the Mekong, and the Yellow (called by Tibetans the Drichu, Dzachu, and Machu, respectively)—run through Tibet and provide water to half the world's population.

The majority of Tibetans live in the eastern reaches of the Tibetan plateau and it's this region that has become the heartland of Tibet, producing famous Tibetan musicians, film directors, writers, activists, and lamas, including the current Dalai Lama.[13]

WHAT DO THE BUDDHA EYES REPRESENT?

"Buddha Eyes"—also called wisdom eyes—can be seen on nearly every stupa or Buddhist shrine in Tibet. Peering out in all four directions, they represent the all-seeing nature of Buddha.

Between the Buddha's eyes is a curly symbol like a question mark that symbolizes the number one, for unity and the path to enlightenment. Above that, the third eye represents the all-seeing wisdom of the Buddha.

In Buddhism everyone is considered to have two types of eyes. The inner eyes see the world of *Dhamma* (also known as the third eye of Buddha); the outer eyes (also known as "material eyes") see the outer world.[14]

Demick goes on to highlight the Tibetan sun, a recurring motif in literary and artistic works because of the way it sweeps the vast plains in illuminating, consuming, and inescapable ways. "Idyllic though Tibet looks in coffee table books, the habitat is brutal to the uninitiated, the weather perilously unpredictable. You can be soaked through the skin one minute, charmed the next by a magnificent double rainbow, then shriveled by ultraviolet rays of the high-altitude sun. Hailstones big as chicken eggs can kill an adult yak and occasionally humans. The oxygen-starved atmosphere leaves newcomers faint and headachy. Even Tibetans get lost in swirling blizzards and die of exposure."[15]

THE CULTURE

Tibetans believe in a fantastical origin myth that their people are descendants of an ape and a cruel warrior ogress who mated on a cliff above a vast inland sea that once covered the Tibetan plateau. The ape was said to be a manifestation of Chenrezig (also known as Avalokiteshvara or Guanyin), the bodhisattva of compassion and the Tibetan patron saint. (Bodhisattvas may be seen as individuals who have chosen to forgo achieving enlightenment in this lifetime in order to help other souls on earth.)

There are also stories of Tibetan people originating from the union of a monkey and a female demon. Both of these tales represent compassion and cruelty, qualities Tibetans believe they inherited.

Tibet's rich and ancient culture is largely based on religion. Buddhist figures are reincarnated over and over, appearing in countless manifestations—male and female, mundane and extravagant—and their statues decorate both spiritual and everyday spaces. What was once an ancient custom of bringing clothes to adorn the statues of deities has become the tradition of offering a white scarf (*kha-btags* or *hada*) symbolizing purity during greetings, visits to shrines, marriage or death ceremonies, and more. Similarly, prayer flags are commonly hung on rooftops, tents, hilltops, and virtually anywhere one wants to ask for fortune and good luck.

Buddhist monasteries have gold-plated roofs that reflect the powerful sun. The structures are painted in deep tones of vermilion and egg-yolk yellow, colors reserved for monastic buildings. On Buddhist holidays there may be a chorus of chanting, clanging of cymbals, and blowing of horns and conch shells as Tibetans chant the *om mani padme hum* to invoke Chenrezig.

OM MANI PADME HUM

Om mani padme hum is a six-syllable mantra that symbolizes purification from a variety of spiritual realms.

- *Om* means freedom from the realm of pride and ego, through generosity.

- The next syllable, *ma*, means purification from jealousy, while *ni* stands for freedom from the realm of passion or desire.

- *Pad* frees people from ignorance and prejudice through diligence.

- The syllable *me* purifies from greed, and the final one, *hum,* frees one from aggression and hatred.

If you were to visit a Tibetan monastery, you would likely see men and women chanting and singing in unison as they push prayer wheels, a ritual called the *kora*. These prayer wheels are big vertical cylinders of metal, wood, and leather—intricately painted works of art complete with mantras and Buddhist symbols, some as large as merry-go-rounds and requiring several people to turn them. Every turn is like reciting the prayer exponentially aloud and sending it out into the ether for all sentient beings.

Tibetan elders may be seen doing repeated circumambulations around a nearby monastery, spinning prayer wheels, or sitting on wooden benches that line courtyards in front of congregation halls, spinning handheld prayer wheels on little spindles. Most older people wear the traditional Tibetan robe, called *chuba*, belted at the waist. Today Tibetans may blend tradition with practicality by donning cowboy hats and sheepskin or puffy down jackets. Women often wear long skirts.

Traditional Tibetan-style homes are made out of rammed earth, dun-colored (gray-gold or tan), that blends into the landscape during the dry season when the plateau is bare of grass. The massive walls taper inward toward the top to provide stability in case of earthquakes. If there is a space dedicated to spiritual practice, it may be vibrant with frescoes and *thang-kas* (religious scroll paintings) in brilliant shades. Tibet is especially renowned for its thang-kas, metal images, and woodblock prints featuring deities in three categories: peaceful, moderate, or angry.

Tibetan marriages traditionally involved consulting with a lama and an astrologer to predict a couple's compatibility. These days, couples are likely to meet at public gatherings. After a couple is officially wed, prayer flags are raised from the rooftop by the bride's family, and everyone participates in a wedding feast.

When there is a death, families make charitable contributions in hopes of ensuring a better realm of reincarnation for the deceased. When an important religious figure dies, the corpse is preserved in a tomb or *stupa* (a Buddhist commemorative structure). Traditional Tibetan funeral practices are described in *Bardo Thödol*—the Tibetan Book of the Dead. It's customary for a corpse to be fed to vultures; this is known as sky burial or celestial burial. Some areas also practice water burial, wrapping the body in white and letting it be carried downstream in a river.[16]

Astrology is an integral part of daily life and decision-making for Tibetans. A combination of Chinese and Indian traditions, it has been used by Tibetans for centuries to gain understanding of themselves, their health, and their fortune.

Tibetan astrology is based on the five elements: space, air, fire, earth, and water. Time acts as a sixth element. As explained on the website of Buddhist master Tulku Lobsang Rinpoche, while we don't have control over these elements, a core Tibetan Buddhist belief is that we are all interconnected—so when the elements move, so do we. If we can know when the elements will be aligned in a certain way, thereby dictating certain behaviors, "we also know how we ourselves will be at that time."[17]

The astrological cycles affect our bodies and the functioning of our organs, so an Eastern medical practitioner takes seasonal changes into account—especially when doing pulse diagnosis. Pulse diagnosis is a common practice in traditional Chinese medicine (TCM), as explained by Kajsa Landgren for *ScienceDirect*. The patient stretches out her wrist as the doctor uses three fingers to take the pulse simultaneously at three places on the wrist. At first only light pressure is used to check one specific organ, and then pressure is increased to check another. Each organ's status is monitored by the quality of the pulse.[18]

Tibetan astrology holds that nothing is random. Superstition is prominent. In fact, as related by Evan Osnos in *The New Yorker*, the 14th Dalai Lama "relies heavily on the 'state oracle,' a deity called Nechung who communicates through a human medium, usually a monk....The Dalai Lama poses questions, and the oracle responds with enigmatic advice.... For further help, the Dalai Lama relies on a form of *mo* divination, in which choices are written on pieces of paper and placed in balls of dough. He then swirls the balls in a cup until the right answer tumbles out."[19]

As Osnos writes, the 14th Dalai Lama balances his trust in science with his faith in the supernatural by viewing these oracles as what he calls "consultants." He says he has made all major decisions from age 16 onward with the help of oracles. When it came to the monumental decision in 1959 whether to stay in Tibet or leave, the oracle–in a trance–drew a route through the mountains, encouraging the Dalai Lama to escape.

Traditionally in Tibet almost all practicing astrologers were Tibetan monks, because in order to have a correct understanding of astrology, deep insight into Buddhist psychology was required. Through mental training as via meditation, astrologists could hone their insights and intuition.

THE TIBETAN CALENDAR

The Tibetan system works with a 360-day lunar year and cycles of 60 and 180 years. Because a year is actually longer than 360 days, some days are doubled and others are skipped—and sometimes a whole month is added!

Certain days of the week and month are considered auspicious for specific activities—whether the hanging of prayer flags, getting married, or cutting one's hair—and every day relates to the specific astrological chart of one's birthday. When a child is born, charts are checked to see if any specific rituals are needed to ward off negative planetary influences. When a person dies, a death chart is prepared to decide the exact rituals of the funeral. It is believed that reading the charts incorrectly could lead to problems for both the family and the deceased.

Unique to Tibet, the "Five Individual Forces" are used for calculating yearly horoscopes. When the forces become weak, specific practices are prescribed to strengthen them again:[20]

- *La*: vitality
- *Sok:* life potential
- *Lu:* bodily health
- *Wangthang:* personal power
- *Lungta:* wind horse or good fortune

Ultimately, Tibetan astrology is a practice of compassion and connectedness. It underscores that we are part of universal cycles, which means it's an illusion to think that we act independently, as we are completely dependent on these cycles and affected by them mentally, physically, and energetically.

TIBETAN MEDICINE

All models of medicine are based on worldviews that reflect underlying beliefs and assumptions about life inherent in the host culture. Thus, to appreciate the inner nature of Tibetan medicine, it's vital to understand that Tibetans believe that the body, mind, and external environment are inextricably intertwined.

Tibetan medicine was first taught more than 2,500 years ago. According to this ancient system, the universe is composed of tiny particles that each contain the qualities and functions of earth, water, fire, and air, interacting in the dimension of the fifth element, space.

Just as the external environment is made of these five elements, so are our bodies. When any of these elements becomes imbalanced (excessive, deficient, or disturbed), then sickness occurs. The goal is to continue bringing these elements into balance.

Here's how this is exhibited in the physical body, as explained in *Tibetan Yoga of Movement* by Chögyal Namkhai Norbu and Fabio Andrico:[21]

- Earth = flesh, muscles, and bones
- Water = liquids, including blood, lymph, and serum
- Fire = catalyst for chemical reactions, such as metabolism, digestion, and bodily heat
- Air = flow of thoughts, breathing
- Space = the openness between the cells, the hollowness of the intestines, and more

Tibetan medicine also identifies three humors or energies that come from various combinations of these elements, similar to the Ayurvedic principles of *vata, pitta,* and *kapha.* Ayurveda (translated as "knowledge of life") is a natural system of medicine that originated in India more than 3,000 years ago.

- Air + space = wind (*lung* or *vata*)
- Fire + water = bile (*tripa* or *pitta*)
- Water + earth = phlegm (*beken* or *kapha*)

How can you achieve a perfect state of health? Keep these three humors in balance. Yet they can become unbalanced so easily that it's believed in Tibetan medicine that we all have unmanifested disease within us. The three humors are also linked to three mental "poisons," negative emotions that cause disease.[22]

Healing the body means healing the mind as well. Tibetan medicine identifies 80 different emotions that can be impacted or elicited by the elements being out of balance, though for simplicity's sake these can be narrowed down to five main negative emotions:

- ❀ Ego-pride
- ❀ Attachment
- ❀ Anger
- ❀ Jealousy
- ❀ Ignorance

When the elements are purified and balanced, these negative emotions become these positive qualities:

- ❀ Devotion and calmness
- ❀ Altruism and selflessness
- ❀ Patience and compassion
- ❀ Appreciation and love
- ❀ Generosity and equanimity

Bodily health depends on our mental state, so it's essential to take care of our happiness. Tibetan wisdom tells us how to care for our bodies and minds.

Having a basic understanding of the elements, humors, and feelings will help as you explore how to coordinate physical movement and breath through the Five Tibetan Rites to produce physical, energetic, mental, and even spiritual benefits. The interdependence of everything in the universe is especially evident in the relationship between Tibetan medicine and Tibetan yoga.

Chapter 3

TIBETAN MOVEMENT PRACTICES

Chime Lama creates concrete poetry, a style in which a poem's visual orientation conveys part or most of its meaning.[23]

TWO TYPES OF TIBETAN YOGA

The Sanskrit term *yoga* means "union," while the Tibetan translation *naljor* more specifically refers to possessing real knowledge of our natural condition, and living—and being—concretely in that wisdom.[24] Exploring the Tibetan movement practices called *'phrul 'khor* can help us better understand the possible origin of the Five Tibetan Rites. There are two specific forms of yoga: *Yantra yoga* and *Trul-Khor*.[25]

YANTRA YOGA

You may have heard of the Yantra yoga from India that's often associated with geometric images. The Yantra yoga of Tibet, on the other hand, was a closely guarded secret for centuries, reserved for advanced yogic practitioners. It originated with an ancient text called *The Unification of the Sun and Moon*, passed down from renowned Tibetan translator Vairochana and a lineage of Tibetan spiritual masters. Tibetan Yantra yoga was first introduced to the West in the 1970s by one of the foremost modern Dzogchen masters, Chögyal Namkhai Norbu.[26] *Dzogchen* is a Tibetan word that means "Great Perfection." Its approach is a universal practice designed to recognize our pure nature, the union of perfect wisdom and perfect compassion.[27]

Yantra yoga has 108 movements, a number highly revered by many spiritual traditions and considered exceptionally auspicious, especially in that it refers to spiritual completion, as well as the fact that in Tibetan Buddhism, the belief is that there are 108 sins and 108 delusions of the mind. The focus of Yantra yoga is on a continuous sequence of movement rather than staying in a position for a long period of time, because the overall movement is what's important. Each position is only a moment in a sequence, guided by the rhythm of breathing and the application of one of five different kinds of breath retention.

This style of yoga is one of the few that authorized teachers will transmit to students who aren't engaged in the traditional three-year retreat process and who haven't completed a lengthy series of prostrations, meditations, and mantras. Currently there's a video from Shang Shung Publications called *The Eight Movements of Yantra Yoga* that Namkhai Norbu was willing to make public and universally accessible, because of his concern that people do the movements properly. The eight movements are considered to be a preparatory method for balancing one's energy system.[28]

Just as with Tibetan astrology and Tibetan medicine, the generations-old practice of Yantra yoga is based on the interdependence of the energies that govern both our inner and outer worlds. The purpose of Yantra yoga is to help maintain our natural condition of peace and harmony.

TRUL-KHOR

Brought to the West by Tenzin Wangyal Rinpoche, a master of the Bön school of the Dzogchen meditative tradition, Trul-Khor means "magical wheel" and consists of seven cycles with a total of 38 movements.[29]

Because of the vigorous and continuous movement, some have compared Trul-Khor to Kundalini yoga, the latter of which uses chanting, singing, breathing exercises, and repetitive poses to activate your Kundalini or Shakti feminine energy (located at the base of your spine). Perhaps this is also why it's thought that the

Five Tibetan Rites originate from Trul-Khor, as they are designed to speed the flow of energy or *prana* up the spine and through the *chakras*, the body's energy vortexes. By combining posture, breath, and motion to create a dynamic energetic effect, the Five Tibetan Rites can generate significant inner power, which can then be used to expand the boundaries of mind and body into a transcendent spiritual state.

THE RISK OF DOING YOGA RIGHT

Teachers of Tibetan yoga must weigh the risk of compromising tradition against the risk that the practices may disappear altogether if not taught more widely. The question becomes how to maintain the original teachings—and if adaptations must be made and the movements aren't practiced as accurately as possible, is it worth it? Because of the belief that the Five Tibetan Rites hold unlimited potential for healing and balancing mind, body, and spirit, these movements were originally considered potentially dangerous to anyone who used them without adequate instruction. In the West, however, the practices are usually not taught to this full capacity, so that risk may be mitigated.

It's important to note that breathing is intimately connected with energy, with the ability to impact your body greater than any type of movement. When playing with the energies of the body, directing or forcing the internal airs into the wrong channels can disrupt the body's natural processes. We'll dive into more deeply into this on page 43.

Ultimately, the intention is to clear your being of unwanted obstructions, imbalances, distractions, or afflictions in order to experience "the natural mind." Various ways to do so are explored throughout this book, applying Tibetan beliefs to a modern lifestyle.

THE SUN AND THE MOON

In Buddhist and Hindu traditions, the two celestial bodies of the sun and the moon symbolize the feminine and masculine aspects of our subtle bodies. In the Himalayan tradition of Buddhism, the male quality is lunar while the female quality is solar. This is a reversal of the Hindu tantric traditions, in which male energy is generally identified as solar and female as lunar.

In Vairochana's Yantra yoga, the solar side is on the right for women and on the left for men, and the goal is to equalize and balance these two energies—ultimately neutralizing the detrimental effects of our fast-paced modern society.

HOW TO ACHIEVE ALIGNMENT

The goal of the Five Tibetan Rites—and generally all Tibetan philosophy—is to live in a state of relaxation, a natural state in the full presence of our potential. In more modern terms, it can also mean living in less hustle and more flow! Combining practices for body, mind, and spirit helps us approach the ups and downs (and all-arounds) of daily life with more peace, calm, and awareness.

Alignment can mean living with integrity according to your core values—however you define them. When it comes to the physical practice of yoga, alignment describes the precise structural way to do any given pose in order to maximize its benefits and minimize the risk of injury. By creating a stable foundation for a safe practice, you allow your body to open in new ways. This can include using supportive props, such as blocks or straps. However, some individuals may find it challenging to adjust practices to fit their own bodies or current mental and emotional state, because the ego-mind equates anything less than "perfect" as similar to inadequacy. The truth is, it requires tremendous strength, bravery, and courage to honor your unique physical self.

Alignment also impacts the subtle energies, the flow of life force (sometimes referred to as *prana* in yoga or *qi* in Eastern medicine) moving through your body. There is life-sustaining prana that allows the formation of consciousness; ascending prana that builds strength and courage; pervasive prana that enables the proper functioning of our orifices; fire-accompanying prana that assimilates nutrients; downward-clearing prana that releases toxins, semen, menstrual fluids, feces, and urine, and is involved in the process of childbirth.[30] By creating an integrated state of alignment in your body, mind, and spirit, you can begin to tap into the harmony at the core of your existence.

The most important of all approaches to alignment may be creating a sense of presence. When you are distracted, whether you are on or off the mat, you are more likely to become injured. By becoming deeply aware of *your* breath, *your* body, and the present moment, you more fully arrive in *your* life.

In the Five Tibetan Rites and the other rituals described in this book, we're playing with the energies of the body. This is when alignment is especially important, because directing or forcing internal air into the wrong channels can disrupt the body's natural processes. Even if done improperly only for a short time, the Five Tibetan Rites could potentially cause insomnia, digestive problems, or even anxiety and depression. Yet if you focus on proper alignment for *your* body and mind, the Five Tibetan Rites can support healing. That's why we'll explore modifications, contraindications, and breathwork in subsequent chapters to ensure that the practice is adapted to *you* and your needs in the moment.

As previously explored, Tibetan medicine identifies five elements—space, air, fire, earth, and water—that correlate with one's body and emotions, positive or negative. The intention is to clear any unwanted obstructions, imbalances, distractions, or afflictions in order to create alignment with "the natural mind." The core purpose of the Five Tibetan Rites is to regulate all the body's functions by tapping into our innate life-force energy. Now let's explore these vortexes—commonly known in yoga as the Hindu chakras—through which your life force spins.

THE SEVEN VORTEXES OR CHAKRAS

The original texts about the Five Tibetan Rites explain that the body contains seven powerfully magnetic energy centers or "vortices" that are invisible to the eye. These were thought to be deep within the forehead; in the posterior part of the brain; at the base of the neck; in the right side of the body at the waist; in the sex organs; in the left knee; and in the right knee.[31]

In subsequent editions, the vortexes are aligned with traditional chakra locations, so those are the areas we'll focus on in the descriptions that follow. Chakras, which means "wheels" in Sanskrit, are a complex and ancient energy system that originated in India and were first mentioned in the Vedas, ancient sacred texts dating from 1500–1000 BC.

Some say there are 114 different chakras, but generally, most yoga practitioners focus on seven main ones.[32] Located along the spinal pathway, each chakra is associated with a particular organ, gland, or nerve plexus, as well as with a certain state of consciousness. According to the Five Tibetan Rites, the speed at which these vortexes are spinning determines your aging process and quality of health. That means that the quickest way to regain youth and vitality is to start these energy centers spinning normally again!

As the primary energetic centers, the seven chakras are the major nexuses of energy distribution for the rest of the human system. They govern the seven ductless glands in the body's endocrine system; the endocrine glands, in turn, regulate all body functions, including the aging process. In a healthy body, each vortex or chakra is open and flowing, allowing for vital life energy (prana) to flow upward through the endocrine system. The chakras are designed to work together, similar to organs, glands, nerves, and other systems of the body. If one or more of them begins to slow down, the flow of vital energy is inhibited or blocked—another name for aging and ill health.

Because the chakras influence every aspect of who you are and how you experience life, the Five Tibetan Rites aim to influence each chakra to function at peak activity, in balance and harmony with each other. When your overall energy system is working well, the body and mind are also healthy, vital, and balanced.

To better understand where these vortexes are in your body and how they can impact you mentally, emotionally, and physically, you can start by learning more about the seven chakras.[33]

1. *Root Chakra.* The first vortex—the root chakra—is located at the base of the spine at the perineum, the spot between the anus and the genitals. *Primary functions:* survival, power, supporting vital life energy; elimination. *Associated organs:* large intestine and rectum. *Associated glands:* adrenal glands.[34]

2. *Sacral Chakra.* The second vortex, or sacral chakra, is in the area of the lower abdomen two inches below the navel, close to the reproductive organs. Since one of the most fundamental acts of human creativity is procreation, the second chakra is the center of sexual energy—more on this in Chapter 4. *Primary functions:* creativity, sense of abundance, pleasure, sexuality; supporting vitality. *Associated organs:* large intestine, bladder, kidneys, reproductive organs. *Associated glands:* reproductive glands.

3. *Solar Plexus Chakra.* The third vortex, the solar plexus chakra, is above the navel in the stomach area, below the chest. As the center of the individual self, the third chakra is the center of personal power

and the origin of will. It's here that we meet the challenges of living in the world through self-assertion, personal determination, and individual strength. *Primary functions:* self-worth, self-confidence, self-esteem; digestion, assimilation of nutrients. *Associated organs:* liver, spleen, stomach, small intestine. *Associated gland:* pancreas.

4. **Heart Chakra.** The fourth vortex or heart chakra is in the center of the chest, just above the heart. Considered the focal point of love and compassion, the fourth chakra is where human consciousness moves beyond self-centeredness into an expanded awareness of connection with the rest of the world. Because this is the midpoint between the three lower and the three higher chakras, it marks the transformation point between lower and higher awareness. *Primary functions:* love, compassion, joy, inner peace; heart, lung, and bronchial functions. *Associated organs:* heart and lungs. *Associated gland:* thymus.

5. **Throat Chakra.** The fifth vortex, the throat chakra, is located in the throat area. Since speaking is an opportunity to express oneself, the throat chakra is associated with communication and personal expression. *Primary functions:* expressing one's feelings or truth; higher creativity. *Associated organs:* vocal cords. *Associated gland:* thyroid.

6. **Brow Chakra.** The sixth vortex or brow chakra is at the center of the forehead, between the eyebrows. Also known as the "third eye" or "wisdom eye," the sixth chakra is related to higher intelligence, insight, and inner vision. *Primary functions:* intuition, imagination, wisdom, ability to think and make decisions, clairvoyance, refined hearing. *Associated organ:* brain. *Associated gland:* pituitary.

7. ***Crown Chakra.*** The seventh, highest vortex—the crown chakra—is at the crown of the head. Many consider this to be the space of absolute awareness and integration with the primary creative force of the universe, also known as cosmic consciousness. However, it requires deep spiritual work and inner refinement to reach this level. *Primary functions:* connection to spirituality, pure bliss. *Associated organ:* brain. *Associated gland:* pineal gland.

THREE MAIN ENERGY PATHWAYS

The seven chakras lie along the spinal column and are connected by three major energetic pathways, known as *ida*, *pingala*, and *sushumna*. All three pathways originate at the base of the spine—the location of the first chakra—and run to the top of the head, conveying energy from one chakra to another.

As the primary pathway, the sushumna is the core channel of all energetic flow in the human energy system, the energetic counterpart to the spinal cord. Kundalini energy, described in Hinduism as a form of divine feminine energy and a sleeping, dormant potential force in the human organism, travels through the sushumna.

Considered lunar in nature, ida runs up the left side of the central channel to the left nostril. Pingala is considered solar in nature, running up the right side of the central channel to the right nostril. These two channels intertwine with each other at each chakra. Their physical counterparts are the ganglionic nerve chains that run alongside the spinal cord.

The Five Tibetan Rites are said to help balance ida and pingala and support a steady, concentrated flow of energy through the sushumna. Each of the Five Tibetan Rites physically stimulates various nerve plexuses and glands along the spinal pathway, as well as the spine itself and the ganglionic nerve chains.

ABOUT BREATHWORK

In Jay Shetty's book *Think Like a Monk*, he describes his first day of monk school, where he noticed a child monk around 10 years old teaching a group of 5-year-olds. When asking the 10-year-old what he was doing and why, Shetty recalls that the young monk explained that breathing is the only constant in life, yet in high-stress situations, your breathing changes. Given that breath is with you throughout your entire life, by learning how to manage your breath, you can then manage any situation you encounter.

Breathwork has increasingly gained popularity in the last few years, thanks to individuals like Dutch extreme athlete Wim Hof, who has challenged conventional ideas of health and healing. Hof has not only accomplished extraordinary feats of human endurance, but he has also scientifically shown that the autonomic nervous system, related to the body's innate immune response, can be willfully influenced. In other words, you have the power to purposefully and positively impact your immune system—something previously unknown to science.[35]

While the original Five Tibetan Rites did not teach breathwork techniques in depth, this book includes several suggested breathwork practices to release more energy, influence your nervous system, and change various physiological responses. This can build resilience to everyday stress and lead to feelings of empowerment.

People may practice breathwork to accomplish any of the following, as outlined on the Healthline website: support positive self-development; boost immunity; process emotions, including healing pain and trauma; develop life skills; increase self-awareness and self-love; deepen a sense of presence, happiness, and joy; improve sleep; reduce stress and anxiety levels; release negative thoughts; and explore altered states of consciousness. Breathwork can also be used to address anger, anxiety, chronic pain, depression, emotional effects of illness, grief, and post-traumatic stress disorder (PTSD).[36]

> ### *Take a Moment to Breathe Right Now*
>
> *Observe what it feels like in your body, mind, and spirit as you bring all of your attention to your inhalation and exhalation.*
>
> *Repeat these simple words as you focus on your breath:*
>
> *In.*
>
> *Out.*
>
> *What do you observe?*

Breathing is both an unconscious process regulated by the autonomic nervous system and also the easiest and most instrumental part of the system that you can control—all through inhalation, exhalation, and retention. The way you breathe has a strong effect on your body's chemical and physiological activities. Breathing meditatively, studies have shown, can actually decrease the size of the amygdala, a part of the brain that triggers the body's fight-or-flight response.[37] What's more, conscious breathing can lower levels of the stress hormone cortisol, high levels of which can cause chronic inflammation. All of this has been linked to aging.[38]

Most disease is caused by stress, and most stress is caused by a mismatch between our beliefs about life and our actual life experiences. We put so much importance on our beliefs because we're convinced they're true. Yet, if our beliefs direct our physiology, then perhaps many of our physical and emotional ailments are the result of our bodies falsely identifying something as true, believing that we are more sick than we are well.

Experts advise approaching breathing exercises with caution, especially if you are purposefully holding your breath through certain physical and mindfulness practices, as this can influence vital energy functions. When you begin practicing the Five Tibetan Rites, see if you can do the breathing exercises on an empty stomach to avoid nausea and cramping and to allow energy to circulate as freely as possible throughout your system.

Breathing is a complete yoga unto itself, so there are hundreds of variations to the practice of pranayama. For those new to breathwork, we'll focus on three specific breathing methods, as recommended by Christopher S. Kilham, author of *The Five Tibetans: Five Dynamic Exercises for Health, Energy, and Personal Power:*[39]

1. Normal breath

2. Long, deep breath

3. Breath performed after each of the Five Tibetans Rites

In our daily lives, we're often distracted by the body being in one place and the mind in another (usually thinking about the past or the future rather than the present). As you become more mindful about your breathing, actively following your inhalation and exhalation, your mind can come back to your body to be more fully present and alive in the here and now. This is the place where you can access a sense of oneness of body and mind.

THE NORMAL BREATH

If you find that you've been breathing in differently than what's suggested below, sucking in your abdomen upon inhaling rather than expanding it, that's okay. In fact, it's very common! Reversing your habitual style of breathing may feel uncomfortable or awkward at first, but continue to try this relaxed pattern as much as possible and observe the effects.

1. Sit in a comfortable position, either cross-legged on the floor or in a straight-backed chair. Keep your spine as tall and aligned as possible, like a stack of gold coins one on top of another. Bring the back of your head in line with the rest of your spine.

2. Relax your shoulders and chest. Place one palm on your abdomen so that you can easily feel what is happening, or gently place your hands on your lap.

3. Breathe in lightly through your nose, letting your abdomen fill and expand outward. Imagine you're filling a balloon—the more you inhale, the more your belly expands. (When inhaling through

the mouth, you bypass breath-regulating mechanisms that help prevent dizziness, nervousness, or other physical and emotional challenges, which is why it's advisable to inhale through the nose.)

4. As you then exhale through your nose or mouth, let your abdomen collapse.

5. Continue practicing this simple and gentle breathwork for about two minutes. Remember to keep expanding your belly on the inhale, releasing on the exhale.

MODERN LIFE TIP: See if you can maintain this style of relaxed breathing throughout the day, whatever experiences may arise.

THE LONG, DEEP BREATH

Similar to the Normal Breath previously described, the Long, Deep Breath invites you to explore your breathwork practice more deeply. In this practice, your breath comes in from the top of your body yet fills the lower abdomen first, then the chest cavity. Practice this breathing regularly until it is easy and automatic.

1. Sit in a comfortable position on the floor or in a straight-backed chair. Begin by placing one palm flat on your abdomen, the other at the center of your chest, so that you can sense the movement of your breath. As with the Normal Breath, this hand placement is simply recommended as you're beginning this practice; you do not need to keep doing this as an ongoing hand position.

2. Breathe in through your nose, filling your abdomen; this time, continue inhaling until your lungs are full to the top and your chest expands.

3. Gently exhale through either your nose or your mouth.

4. Continue practicing this breathing for several minutes.

MODERN LIFE TIP: You can do this exercise whenever you need to alleviate stress, as a method to release tension and leave you feeling calm, relaxed, and maybe even invigorated. Just avoid doing it after eating a large meal when the physical focus is on digestion.

THE INTERIM BREATH

This exercise is specifically designed to be performed two times after each of the Five Tibetan Rites.

1. Stand straight with your feet close together and your hands on your hips.

2. Take a long, deep breath, inhaling through your nose.

3. Exhale through your mouth with your lips pursed in an "O."

MODERN LIFE TIP: Take a few minutes to practice the Interim Breath now, so that you'll be familiar with it when you begin the Rites.

Chapter 4

THE FIVE TIBETAN RITES

The New Beginning

To love you is to mediate
To mediate is to dissolve
To dissolve is to extend
To extend is to grow,
To grow is to live
To live is to love
To love is to mediate ...
The essence of life is in its possibility
The greatest possibility of life is to be in love.

—Tenzing Rigdol[40]

It's important to be diligent when practicing the Five Tibetan Rites
or even applying various facets of Tibetan Buddhist beliefs. Because
one of the Buddhist principles is to attain a favorable rebirth, while
understanding that most individuals will not achieve enlightenment

in one lifetime, persevering with your practice can help keep you focused on your goals.

Evan Osnos, in *The New Yorker*, describes that the Dalai Lama wakes up most mornings at 3:30 am. He begins the day by meditating, then follows with full-body prostrations that are both exercise and ritual. He'll walk outside, have breakfast at 5:30 am, and listen to the radio. Soon he'll return to meditation, read about philosophy, have a day full of work and meetings and another hour or two of meditation before going to bed at 8:30 pm.

Wise teachers say that you can't *find* time to meditate, but rather you have to *make* time. In the same way, see if you can *make* time for your practice of the Five Tibetan Rites. The good news is that you can perform the Rites anytime, anywhere. The most important thing to remember is to fit this practice to your unique physical requirements—and into your mental, emotional, and spiritual journey—so that it becomes part of your overall lifestyle.

The following are a few suggestions to support your experience. How will you begin *your* practice of the Five Tibetan Rites? What will your routine look like on most days?

CHOOSE YOUR TIME OF DAY

It's optimal to practice in the morning before breakfast or in the evening before going to bed. However, some people feel more energized after performing the Five Tibetan Rites, so you may find it counterproductive to practice before bed as it would wind you up rather than down. Try the Five Tibetan Rites out for yourself and see what works for you, understanding that every day is different, so what you need in this moment may be different as well.

PAY ATTENTION

By bringing a sense of ritual or attentiveness to your practice, you can create your own personal sanctuary. Perhaps you'd like to light a candle or incense, wash your hands or face, say a mantra, set an intention, write in your journal, meditate, or do a little movement—even dancing! Whatever you choose, you can make the Five Tibetan Rites a special experience every day.

PRACTICE ON AN EMPTY STOMACH

Experts recommend practicing the Five Tibetan Rites approximately two hours after your previous meal, since the digestive process requires energy. The aim is to increase the flow of vital life energy, and practicing when you're not digesting lets your body direct energy where it's needed. When food is in the digestive tract, your body uses blood and circulatory energy to absorb nutrients and produce hormones, enzymes, and chemicals, all to manage the digestive process. Yoga poses and breathwork take energy away from the digestive system, which limits your body's ability to digest. What's more, you might experience nausea, bloating, or gas during practice if you've recently eaten.

If you're hungry and need a little something prior to practicing the Five Tibetan Rites, eat a small portion of an easily digestible food (such as a banana) about 30 minutes before doing the movements. This small snack can make its way through your system quickly to help avoid adverse effects during your practice.

CHOOSE COMFORTABLE CLOTHING AND ANY PROPS YOU NEED

Traditionally the Five Tibetan Rites are practiced on a densely woven rug about the size of a yoga mat. But you really don't need any special equipment to begin. A normal yoga mat or even the bare floor is fine. If you're looking to purchase a mat and want optimal support, look for a thick mat that's firm, resilient, and (ideally) produced with nontoxic sustainable materials. You can also use cushions or other props for added comfort and support.

When it comes to clothing, you'll want to wear loose, nonrestrictive clothing that allows for total freedom of movement, preferably made of light, breathable materials such as organic cotton, hemp, linen, or bamboo.

SET THE SPACE

If possible, create a space designated solely for doing the Five Tibetan Rites and your yoga, mindfulness, and breathing practice. Find a pleasant, spacious, clean place that's well ventilated and neither too hot nor too cold.

Let your practice become a special time devoted to your personal health and well-being, as well as an opportunity to honor and respect yourself. The most important element is to become more present with yourself, experiencing a sense of gratitude that you have shown up for every moment of your life thus far—because you have indeed made it through every single one of the hardest moments of your life. Good for you for beginning.

HOW TO PRACTICE THE FIVE TIBETAN RITES

The Five Tibetan Rites stimulate full energy flow through the chakras and enliven corresponding nerves, organs, and glands. You'll also tone and strengthen major muscle groups by doing these movements. But at the heart of it all is a sense of compassion for who you are now and who you are endeavoring to become.

Once you're familiar with the Five Tibetan Rites, practicing them will take only about five to 10 minutes a day. However, let's start with a few important caveats!

As with any exercise regimen, please consult first with a physician and make any modifications necessary for your unique body. No book can cover all the potential effects that might arise when you perform certain movements, or offer in-depth advice on how to develop the Five Tibetan Rites to your own fullest capacity, so it's highly recommended that you seek an experienced teacher to guide you in developing your practice. This is especially true if you have a medical condition or any doubts about doing certain exercises, or if you are pregnant. If you are menstruating, yoga teachers generally advise that you avoid inverted positions and approach strong holds with less intensity.

Cautions, contraindications, and suggested modifications have been included in the following pages; even with such adjustments, you can still experience the same benefits. Whatever your body type, age, or flexibility, know that there are myriad ways to experience substantial benefits for your mind, body, and spirit.

Be patient and compassionate with yourself as you learn to coordinate the movements of the Five Tibetan Rites with breathwork and mindfulness. As shared by Emily and Amelia Nagoski, authors of *Burnout: The Secret to Unlocking the Stress Cycle*, in an interview with Brené Brown: "Wellness is not a state of being, it is a state of action. It's the freedom to oscillate. There is no gold at the end of the rainbow. The rainbow is the gold."[41]

A FEW MORE NOTEWORTHY BITS

Remember that you are the only one in relationship with your body, energy, and mind, so only you can be responsible for your practice. Use as many modifications as are right for you.

- Be as fully present as possible, remembering that distractions lead to a higher likelihood of injuries. Consider every movement progress and do not try to force things.

- Free your mind from obstacles and limitations, giving yourself an opportunity to return to your true and natural condition. Start slowly and work up to 21 repetitions over time. To ensure you have enough time, try to wake up earlier or go to bed later. You can also combine the Five Tibetan Rites with other exercise programs. It's thought that the Rites help normalize the chakras, so your body becomes even more receptive to the benefits of exercise.

- Allow your breathing to support your movement. Rather than force or strain your body or your breathing, approach your practice with a focused yet relaxed attitude. Afterward, stand with your feet shoulder-width apart and take a full cycle of breath to ground yourself.

❋ Be mindful of your head and neck, particularly when it comes to the speed and extension of any of the Five Tibetan Rites. Maintain elongation of the front and back of your neck during any movement of transferring chin to chest or extending toward the back of the body.

❋ Be as fully present as possible. Try turning off your phone to avoid distractions. When you are distracted, you're more likely to get injured. Instead of trying to overcome limitations by forcing things, be gentle with yourself. The more aware you are, the more you can lean into your growing edge without straining.

❋ Reflect upon your alignment on all levels—physically, mentally, emotionally, and spiritually, including observing your subtle energies. The goal is to harmonize your entire being.

ORIGINAL TIPS FROM PETER KELDER

Kelder's original book, *The Eye of Revelation*, suggests practicing the Five Tibetan Rites daily in order to achieve real benefits. He says that you can skip one day a week, but try not to miss more than that.[42]

When you begin, it will take about 21 minutes to complete all five Rites; as you become more adept and physically fit, you should be able to complete the entire series in five to 10 minutes.

Kelder reminds us that it's important to pay attention to mental attitude and intention. Because the Five Tibetan Rites are designed to help achieve optimal health, your mindset makes a significant difference in the results you'll see. If you set an intention of thriving in your life, you can indeed create the results you'd like to see— as demonstrated by the science of epigenetics (how behaviors and environment can change the way genes work) and health innovators such as Dutch athlete Wim Hof (see page 43).

HOW MANY TIMES SHOULD YOU DO EACH RITE?

Ideally, each of the Five Tibetan Rites is repeated 21 times. Most people need to work up to this number, so be gentle with yourself. Many beginners take a month or longer to work up to the full number of repetitions.

As a suggested beginner schedule, practice each of the Five Tibetan Rites just three times a day for the first week. You can even split this into two sessions—morning and evening—to fit your schedule. Increase the daily repetitions by two every week until you're performing each Rite 21 times a day.

One of the most important things to remember is that under no circumstances should you ever strain yourself—this would be counterproductive! If you feel your ego pulling you to do more and go harder, it can be helpful to turn to the Tibetan Buddhist idea of compassion and avoid becoming discouraged. Instead, give yourself a heaping dose of time and patience to adapt the practices to fit your body. Simply do as much as you can and build up gradually. As Kelder notes, there are very few people who, if disciplined, cannot eventually perform all five Rites.

According to Kelder's interview with Bradford nearly a century ago, "These Rites are so powerful…that if one were left out, while the other four were practiced regularly the full number of times, excellent results would still be experienced…so if you find that you simply cannot perform all of the Rites or that you cannot perform them the full twenty-one times, be assured that you will get good results from whatever you are able to do."[43]

In Kelder's original work, he offered two additional tips:

- Pay attention to maintaining deep rhythmic breathing while resting in between each Rite. Stand quietly with your hands on your hips, breathing deeply and rhythmically several times. As you exhale, imagine that you are releasing any tension in your body to feel more relaxed and at ease. As you breathe in, imagine that you are replenishing yourself with radiant life-force energy. (Alternatively, this would be an ideal opportunity to practice the Interim Breath as noted on page 48.)

- Take a cool bath (not a cold one) after completing the Rites to avoid chilling yourself internally, which would undo all the benefits you've just gained. You can also go over your entire body with a wet towel, then follow that with a dry one.

Let this be a transformative experience, one that coordinates and frees your life energy. Are you ready to discover more of who you truly are?

GENERALLY HELPFUL SUGGESTIONS

Roeshan Shadravan is an integrative practitioner, an osteopath with European training, and an educator who holds a doctorate in naprapathic medicine, a doctorate in osteopathic clinical studies, and a master of science in athletic therapy. The following are her suggestions for doing the Five Tibetan Rites. She has also shared her expertise in each of the Cautions, Contraindications, and Mindful Modifications sections for the Five Tibetan Rites.

Remember—it's advisable to consult with your physician prior to beginning any exercise program.

PAY SPECIAL ATTENTION TO TRANSITIONS

Because the Rites are dynamic, be mindful when performing transitions, paying special attention to your breath and your stance. Pause for as many breaths as needed, especially if any dizziness persists.

BE ESPECIALLY CAREFUL IF...

If you are experiencing any of the following, please consult your primary care physician before beginning the Five Tibetan Rites. Be extra mindful when performing any of the Rites, and consider using the modified version of each movement.

- Abdominal surgery within last six months
- Amyloidosis
- Arrhythmia
- Carotid sinus syndrome
- Cerebrovascular disease
- Chronic fatigue
- Enlarged heart/heart valve problems
- Fibromyalgia
- Heart attack within the last three months
- Hernia
- Hypertrophic cardiomyopathy
- Hypothyroidism
- Meniere's disease
- Menstruation (as noted on page 53, it's helpful to be mindful during your monthly cycle when practicing the Five Tibetan Rites)
- Multiple sclerosis
- Orthostatic hypotension
- Parkinson's disease

- Pulmonary stenosis

- Seizure

- Severe arthritis of the spine

- Spinal disc diseases

- Subclavian stenosis

- Untreated high blood pressure

- Vasovagal syncope

- Vertigo

- Wernicke encephalopathy

TIBETAN RITE ONE

The first Rite is designed to speed up the vortexes and get your energy open, flowing, and balanced. Think about how children play—they're naturally spinning and dancing and moving their bodies. Let's return to a sense of that whirling joy within ourselves!

Make sure the space is clear around you, in case of a fall, and keep your eyes open. At first most adults will be able to spin around only half a dozen times or fewer before becoming quite dizzy. If you feel like sitting or lying down to recover from your dizziness, please do so.

IS THIS WHAT WHIRLING DERVISHES DO?

Renowned mystic poet Jalaluddin Rūmī Balkhi—known as Rūmī—is said to have been in a bazaar one day when he heard rhythmic pounding by goldbeaters that sounded to him like *La ilaha illallah*—"There is no God except God," the Islamic declaration of faith.

Being enraptured in divine love, he began whirling with the rhythm, giving birth to the Sufi musical tradition *sema*— translated as "listening," or what is seen today as a physically active meditation. This then gained international recognition through the Raqs, the dance of the whirling dervishes. A dervish whirls counterclockwise, unlike the movement of Tibetan Rite One. One hand is raised, signifying the receiving of divine mercy; the other hand is lowered to bless all of creation.

It is only after intense spiritual and musical training that the dervishes can qualify to participate in sema. The ceremony is led by a *sheikh* (master), whose hand is kissed by each dervish before they commence their dance and features recitation of Qur'anic verses.[44]

CAUTIONS. If you are experiencing any of the following, be extra cautious about moving forward with the Five Tibetan Rites and consider avoiding this pose altogether:

- Brachial plexus syndromes

- Carpal tunnel

- Cervical neuralgia

- Pinched nerve in the cervical spine

- Syncope

- Thoracic outlet syndrome

- TMD (temporomandibular joint disorder)

CONTRAINDICATIONS. If you are experiencing any of the following, it is best not to attempt this Rite:

- Enlarged heart; heart valve problems

- Heart attack within the last three months

- Inability to stand in an upright position

- Meniere's disease

- Multiple sclerosis

- Parkinson's or similar diseases

- Pregnancy with symptoms of nausea

- Seizure disorders

- Vertigo

INSTRUCTIONS

1. Stand erect with arms outstretched to your sides, horizontal to the floor.

2. Without wandering from your starting spot, slowly spin around from left to right, the way the hands on a clock move, until you feel

slightly dizzy. As you do the Rite, lengthen from your shoulders to your fingers through the whole hand, including your fingertips and fingernails.

TIPS. With time, as you practice all the Rites, you'll be able to spin more with less dizziness. To lessen your dizziness, do what dancers and figure skaters do—focus on a single point straight ahead. As you start to turn, hold your vision on that point for as long as you can. Eventually you will have to let it leave your field of vision so that your head can spin on around. Turn your head quickly and refocus on that same point as soon as you can.

In contrast to the Persian or Turkish tradition of whirling dervishes who focus on continuous spinning for prolonged periods, the Five Tibetan Rites are designed to be done just enough to stimulate the vortexes, or chakras, into action.

MINDFUL MODIFICATIONS

- If you have difficulty recovering after Rite One, decrease the rate, speed, or number of reps—especially if you experience headache, nausea, loss of balance, lightheadedness, or dizziness.

- If you have TMD or extreme tension in the upper back, neck, or base of the skull, maintain a slight spread in your fingers, since closed fingers tighten the jaw. The more neutral and not overstretched your fingers are, the more you can get the base of your skull and your jaw to soften.

- If you have brachial plexus, carpal tunnel, thoracic outlet, or any numbing or tingling in the arms or fingers, angle your arms downward and slightly forward.

If you have shoulder, elbow, or wrist issues, face your palms forward when you spin; reach equally from the crown of your head through your arms, lengthen both arms equally, and maintain a slight bend in your elbows.

TIBETAN RITE TWO

Rite Two is designed to further stimulate the seven vortexes, or chakras. According to Eastern philosophies, everything in our lives originates within us as individuals. By looking within—even closing your eyes—you can reflect upon what illusions and stories you tell yourself, including those about health and aging.

CAUTIONS. If you are experiencing any of the following, be extra cautious about moving forward with the Five Tibetan Rites, and consider avoiding this pose altogether:

- Chronic fatigue
- Fibromyalgia
- Gastroparesis
- High blood pressure

- Hip flexor dysfunction

- Menstruating at present

- Multiple sclerosis

- Parkinson's disease

- Rectus diastasis

- Shoulder issues

- Sacroiliac joint issues

- Ulcers

CONTRAINDICATIONS. If you are experiencing any of the following, it is best not to attempt this Rite:

- Neck or lower back pain or stiffness

- Increase in TMD symptoms

- Headaches

- Pregnancy

INSTRUCTIONS

1. Lie flat on the floor, face up, preferably on a yoga mat or a wool rug, as traditionally used during Eastern yoga practices.

2. Fully extend your arms out to your sides and place your palms against the floor, keeping your fingers close together.

3. Tuck your chin to your chest as you raise your head off the floor; simultaneously lift your legs, keeping them straight, into a vertical position, so that your body becomes shaped like an "L" on the floor.

If you can, extend your legs over your body toward your head; do not let your knees bend.

4. Slowly lower both your head and legs to the floor, keeping your knees straight. Let your muscles relax; then repeat. (If you're unable to keep your knees completely straight, let them bend as much as you need to. Straighten them as much as you can as you continue to perform the Rite.)

5. With each repetition, establish a breathing rhythm. Breathe in deeply as you lift your legs and head; breathe out fully as you lower them.

6. Between repetitions, while letting the muscles relax, keep breathing in the same rhythm. The more deeply you breathe, the better.

MINDFUL MODIFICATIONS

- *For shoulder/neck issues*: rotate your arms so that your palms face your thighs, thumbs pointing toward the sky and pinky side down.

- *For back issues*: keep your legs hip-distance apart, maintain a slight bend in your knees, and maintain a neutral pelvis—neither curving forward nor tilting backward.

- *For neck and upper back issues*: untuck your chin and elongate your neck equally through front and back, supporting your cervical spine, through the crown of your head.

TIBETAN RITE THREE

The lamas believe that in addition to creating material change, you can actually begin to shift your reality starting on the astral plane, high above the vibrations of the physical world. To engage these subtle vibrations, start by focusing on a powerful focal point within.

MINDFUL NOTES. Practice Rite Three immediately after you do Rite Two. You can close your eyes as you perform this Rite. Place a yoga block between your knees to maintain stability and alignment of your legs, hips, and lower back.

CAUTIONS. If you are experiencing any of the following, be extra cautious about moving forward with the Five Tibetan Rites and consider avoiding this pose altogether:

- ⚙ Chronic neck or lower back issues
- ⚙ Plantar fasciitis
- ⚙ Screws, plates, pins, or fused joints in the feet or ankles, or foot surgeries

CONTRAINDICATIONS. If you are experiencing any of the following, it is best not to attempt this Rite:

- 🏵 Anterolisthesis

- 🏵 Cervical fibromyalgia

- 🏵 Disc herniations

- 🏵 Migraine

- 🏵 Pregnancy

- 🏵 Sacroiliac joint issues

- 🏵 Whiplash

INSTRUCTIONS

1. Kneel on a mat or rug on the floor with your knees bent and the trunk of your body erect. Your hands should be placed at arm's length against your thigh muscles on the side.

2. Incline your head and neck forward, tucking your chin against your chest. Gently untuck your chin and move your head and neck backward as far as you can and then lean backward, arching your spine and bracing your arms and hands against your thighs for support. This pose most commonly resembles the "Camel" pose.

3. Return to your original position and start over again.

4. Establish a rhythmic breathing pattern, breathing in deeply as you arch your spine and breathing out as you return to an erect position. Deep breathing is beneficial, so take as much air into your lungs as you can.

MINDFUL MODIFICATIONS

🌸 *For knee issues*: add extra padding under your knees or toes; keep your knees and feet hip-distance apart.

🌸 *For back/neck issues*: place your hands on your hips and engage your glutes; keep your neck neutral, maintaining length in both front and back; reach the crown of your head and your tailbone away from each other; anchor your tailbone toward the ground; refrain from bowing your head too far forward or back—especially if you have pain, headache, or nausea.

🌸 *For dizziness*: keep your eyes open and choose a focal point to look at, such as the tip of your nose.

TIBETAN RITE FOUR

Rite Four is designed to continue supporting you as you return to your natural state of mind and purify your life force, by aligning and expanding your vital energy in a relaxed way.

CAUTIONS. If you are experiencing any of the following, be extra cautious about moving forward with the Five Tibetan Rites and consider avoiding this pose altogether:

🌸 Pain in the wrists, shoulders, neck, or lower back

🌸 Screws, pins, plates, or fused joints in the foot or ankle

CONTRAINDICATIONS. If you are experiencing any of the following, it is best not to attempt this Rite:

- ❀ Acute herniations
- ❀ Annular tears
- ❀ Arthrodesis
- ❀ Injuries or surgeries that don't allow for this range of motion
- ❀ Pregnancy
- ❀ Pelvic upslip or sacroiliac joint issues

INSTRUCTIONS

1. If you'd like, you can close your eyes to perform this Rite. Sit on the floor on a mat or a rug with your legs straight out in front of you and your feet about shoulder-width apart; you can place a yoga block between your knees to maintain stability and alignment of legs, hips, and low back. Keep your spine long and erect as you press your palms on the floor alongside your hips, fingers pointing toward your toes. Tuck your chin forward against your chest.

2. Untuck your chin, letting your head sink back as far as it will go. Keep your arms straight and your hands and feet in place as you press into the ground, bend your knees, and lift your hips toward the sky. This is commonly known as the "Reverse Table-Top" pose. Keep your neck in line with the rest of your spine. Tense every muscle in your body, then take a full cycle of breath.

3. Relax your muscles as you return to your original sitting position. Rest for a full cycle of breath before repeating the Rite.

4. Breathing is important for this Rite: breathe in deeply as you raise your body. Hold your breath as you tense your muscles, and then breathe out completely as you come down. As you rest between repetitions, continue breathing in the same rhythm.

MINDFUL MODIFICATIONS

- *For back/neck issues*: keep your neck neutral, maintaining equal elongation for front and back reaching up through the crown. Be mindful to not whip your head, and maintain elongation of front and back while transferring your chin to your chest to full extension. Refrain from bowing your head too far forward or backward if you experience pain, headache, or nausea. Reach your head and pelvis away from each other as you anchor your tailbone toward the ground and engage your glutes.

- *For wrist/joint issues*: engage your glutes to protect your lower back and press the ground away with your fingertips out. Maintain a small bend in your elbows and press firmly through thumb and fingertips to avoid sinking into the heel of your hand; you can make your hands into fists for this pose.

TIBETAN RITE FIVE

By making a conscious effort, you can correct any imbalances in your life-force energy, namely the way ailments, disease, and discomfort are expressed in your body, breath, and mind. Be mindful of your alignment and movement; observe your inhalation, exhalation, and retention. Aim to maintain a state of relaxed concentration as you perform this Rite.

CAUTIONS. If you are experiencing any of the following, be extra cautious about moving forward with the Five Tibetan Rites, and consider avoiding this pose altogether:

- Pain in the wrists, shoulders, neck, or lower back
- Screws, pins, plates, or fused joints in your feet, ankles, hands, or wrists

CONTRAINDICATIONS. If you are experiencing any of the following, it is best not to attempt this Rite:

- Low blood pressure
- Pregnancy
- Surgeries that don't allow for this range of motion

INSTRUCTIONS

1. Lie facedown on the floor on a mat or a rug. Throughout this Rite, your hands should be palm-down against the floor and your feet should be in a flexed position, toes pressed to the floor. Feet and hands should be about shoulder-width apart, and arms and legs should be straight.

2. Lift your body so that your arms are straight, perpendicular to the floor, and your spine is arched so that your body is in a sagging position. This is commonly known as the "Upward Facing Dog" pose. Aim to keep your legs straight. Gently move your head backward as far as you can.

3. Bending at the hips, now raise your body up into an inverted V position, also known as the "Downward Facing Dog" pose. At the same time, bring your chin forward and down, tucking it against your chest.

4. Return to your original position and begin the Rite over again.

TIPS. By the end of the first week, most people will find Rite Five one of the easiest to perform. Once you become proficient, let your body drop from the raised position to a point almost, but not quite, touching the floor. Tense your muscles for a moment at both the raised point and the low point. Follow the same deep-breathing pattern used for all the previous Rites—breathe in deeply as you raise your body, and breathe out fully as you lower it.

MINDFUL MODIFICATIONS

- When you're in the pose resembling "Upward Facing Dog," as you're lying on your stomach with your arms by your ribs, pushing the ground away with your legs long behind you, remember to lift up your pelvis, draw your chest and gaze forward, and keep your neck neutral. Elongate both front and back of the neck. Draw the heels of your hands back and lean your chest forward. Lightly draw your navel toward your spine, tighten your glutes, and simultaneously stretch your head and heels away from one another.

- In the pose resembling "Downward Facing Dog," where your body becomes an inverted "V," bend your knees slightly and reach your head and tailbone away from each other through the length of your spine, ears in line with your upper arms to create a neutral neck. Press down equally through your fingertips and palms to avoid excess weight in the wrists or excessive strain in the heels of your hands.

- Lengthen through your elbows without hyperextending.

ONE ADDITIONAL TIBETAN RITE

Kelder describes one additional Rite for completely restoring full health, vitality, and youth—yet there's a reason he saves it for last. Rite Six, as shared with Kelder by Bradford, involves the kind of difficult self-restraint and restriction that most people would not want to pursue. Designed to lift up reproductive energy—both in body and in mind—it requires you to be celibate.

Many religious and spiritual traditions regard sexual activity as a distraction from "higher" pursuits, believing that fulfilling such desires is the antithesis to pursuits of the soul. Yet, there's a contrasting opinion that physical intimacy and connection are an incredibly normal part of being human!

For the average man or woman, a large part of vital life-force energy is channeled into reproductive energy, dissipated in the lower chakras or vortexes, which means this life-force energy never has a chance to reach the higher ones. Kelder suggests *transmuting* this powerful urge instead and simultaneously lifting it upward. "In this way," he writes, "you have not only discovered the *elixir of life*, as the ancients called it, you have also put it to use, which is something the ancients were seldom able to do."[45]

In other schools of thought, some believe that Rite Six actually allows for a strengthening of the sex glands, thereby enhancing sexual activity. However you view it, whether you choose to practice celibacy or not, it's worthwhile learning more about this Rite.

In Kelder's original text, you're cautioned not to attempt Rite Six unless you are genuinely motivated. What's more, to successfully perform this Rite, you *must* still have an active sexual urge, since you cannot transmute reproductive energy if there's nothing there to work with. But if you're really struggling against your desire for sexual expression, then you're not truly capable of transmuting reproductive energy and directing it upward. Instead, the energy will be misdirected into struggle and inner conflict. As Kelder says, "The sixth rite is only for those who feel sexually complete and who have a real desire to move on to different goals."[46]

For most people, a celibate life simply isn't feasible. But never say never! After performing the other Rites, you may change your mind and have a genuine desire to take your practice to the next level. If you do choose this path, Kelder cautions that once you go forward, you must not look back. The following instructions are how to transmute the energy in Rite Six.

CAUTIONS. If you are experiencing the following, be extra cautious about moving forward with the Five Tibetan Rites and consider avoiding this pose altogether:

- Low blood pressure or prone to fainting

CONTRAINDICATIONS. If you are experiencing any of the following, it is best not to attempt this Rite.

- Pregnancy
- Vasovagal syncope

INSTRUCTIONS

Rite Six should be practiced only when you feel strong sexual energy. Repeat this exercise a maximum of three times to redirect sexual energy and turn its powerful force upward. Here's what to do:

1. Stand up straight with your hands on your hips and your feet about hip-distance apart. Take a long, full inhalation through the nose.

2. Bend forward, hands on your knees, as you exhale through your mouth with your lips pursed in an "O." Slowly let all the air out of your lungs.

3. Force out the last trace of air and hold your breath for several seconds.

4. With your lungs now empty, take in a long, slow, deep breath and return to a straight-up posture.

5. With your feet together and your hands on your hips, take two full, deep breaths, inhaling through the nose and exhaling through the mouth.

Chapter 5

DIVE DEEPER INTO TIBET'S SPIRITUAL HISTORY

Offering Farewell Prostrations
Wings of the heart stretch across space
Where the strong wind howls in its borders.
Alone I stand stiff near the river
Raising my hands high to signal
That if in time I do not go back
I'll sleep forever in this riverbed
Where my flesh and bones become offerings
To nourish budding trees and blossoming flowers.
—Khawa Nyingchak[47]

CHALLENGES WITH CHINA

There's a key principle in Tibetan etiquette that whenever you leave home, you ensure it is a respectful, peaceful, and calm experience. This was not so in 1959 when, after a failed anti-Chinese uprising, the 14th Dalai Lama had to flee Tibet to set up a government-in-exile in India.

Tibet has had a tumultuous history, at times independent and at others ruled by powerful Chinese and Mongolian dynasties. In modern times, China has governed Tibet since 1950, requiring foreigners to obtain a special travel permit to visit the Tibet Autonomous Region. Though the world often sees Tibet as a land of pacifists, historically they were also forceful nomads who ventured across central Asia, subduing other peoples into the Tibetan nation. The Tibetan empire collapsed in the mid-ninth century, and it was not until 1642 that a strong, centralized Tibet was reestablished under the leadership of a succession of Dalai Lamas, supported by the Mongols.[48]

Many Tibetans feel an allegiance to the exiled spiritual leader, the Dalai Lama or Ocean of Wisdom (*dalai* is Mongolian for "ocean" and *lama* is "teacher" in Tibetan). He is seen by his followers as a living god. March 10 is a symbolic date marking what Tibetans believe was the beginning of their exile. Every year on this day, Tibetans in exile stage demonstrations.

After fleeing Tibet in 1959, the Dalai Lama settled in a mountaintop village called McLeod Ganj, outside Dharamsala in the northern part of India. About 300 miles north of New Delhi, Dharamsala was once a cantonment for British military troops in the region. With its auspicious Hindi name, "dwelling place of dharma," the area appealed to Tibetans, who also liked its relatively cool temperatures and mountain air—despite the fact that it didn't much resemble Tibet. Thankfully, the snow-capped Himalayas were visible in the distance. About 80,000 Tibetans followed the Dalai Lama to exile in India in 1959, with a resurgence of emigrants in the 1980s. Today Dharamsala is the capital for more than 150,000 Tibetans in exile worldwide.

One of the challenges of Tibet's theocratic system of government is that the head of state is appointed through reincarnation. A new leader therefore cannot be born until the old one dies, which requires a long transition before the next leader (always a boy) is identified and raised to adulthood. The current Dalai Lama is working on changing this system.

In 1995, a 6-year-old boy named Gedhun Choekyi Nyima was identified and endorsed by the Dalai Lama as the reincarnation of the 10th Panchen Lama, who had died in 1989. (The Panchen Lama is the second-most-important figure in Tibetan Buddhism.) But, Beijing refused to acknowledge Gedhun Choekyi Nyima, naming its own Panchen Lama, Gyaltsen Norbu. Within three days of his appointment, Nyima was detained by Chinese authorities and subsequently disappeared from public view. The Chinese government claims that he is living a normal life and that his parents are both employed by the state. Yet they won't provide details—to protect him, they say, from being "kidnapped by separatists." Nyima's disappearance has challenged the Dalai Lama's lineage, and many believe Beijing hopes to install its own Dalai Lama when the current incarnation passes away.[49]

LOOKING AHEAD

In 2011 the Dalai Lama officially retired as head of the exile government, giving up his leadership to an elected prime minister, ending centuries of theocratic rule. Today Tibetans are debating about whether the institution of the Dalai Lama should continue at all. The 14th Dalai Lama has indicated that he might select his own reincarnation while still alive, a process known as *madhey tulku*. That would give him the chance to train a successor and avoid the gap in leadership that has always been a time of instability for Tibetans.

Meanwhile, many Tibetans now focus on maintaining the freedom to preserve their culture, memories, and language, both inside and outside of China. In Dharamsala, the Library of Tibetan Works and Archives holds more than 100,000 Tibetan-language titles.[50]

TIBETAN SPIRITUALITY

Note: In Mahayana Buddhism, Dharmakaya is the ultimate nature of the fully enlightened mind, a union of pure appearance and emptiness.[51]

BÖN AND BUDDHISM

When you imagine Tibet, you may think of monks in maroon and saffron robes, or carnivals of color. Because Tibetan Buddhism is such a strong element in both monastic and everyday communities, there's an emphasis on such outwardly religious activities as ritual practice at temples, pilgrimages, personal or public prayer wheels, flags, festivals, and ceremonies.

Tibetan Buddhism became a major influence toward the end of the eighth century, when it was brought from India at the invitation of Tibet's king, Trisong Detsen. (It had originally been brought over in the seventh century under King Songtsen Gampo, but the practice then was centered in the royal court and not greatly accessible.) King Detsen asked two Buddhist masters—Shantarakshita and Padmasambhava—to visit the region and translate important Buddhist texts into Tibetan. Shantarakshita, abbot of Nalanda in India, built the first monastery in Tibet.

Today three distinct religious traditions are commonly practiced by Tibetans:

1. The divine dharma, or Buddhism

2. Bön dharma, the native pre-Buddhist religious tradition of Tibet

3. The dharma of human beings, or folk religion[52]

Bön is a system of shamanistic and animistic practices performed by priests (called *shen* or *bonpo*), as explained by John Powers in the book *Introduction to Tibetan Buddhism*. Bön holds that every part of nature is alive with forces that make up the sky, the sea, the soil, and everything else in between.

Tibetans naturally seek local shamans to perform rituals for either protection or luck. Supernatural beings are still prominent in Tibetan Buddhism—both godlike and wrathful deities abound. In fact, the Dalai Lama himself consults with a "state oracle" (see page 27).

In its earliest form, Buddhism was nontheistic (not involving a belief in god or gods), which meant that its focus was more on a way of thinking and a way of life that would release human beings from inevitable suffering and lead to spiritual liberation. As Buddhism became more pervasive in the region, Tibetans increasingly adopted the teachings of Mahayana Buddhism, infused with tantric, shamanic, and Bön influences. Mahayana Buddhism is one of two major Buddhist traditions that emerged around the first century AD and is typically focused on altruistically oriented spiritual practice as embodied in the ideal of the bodhisattva.

THE DALAI LAMA AND REINCARNATION

Buddhists believe that our body is on loan to us, so our experience in this life is fleeting. Our immortal soul goes through many incarnations, which means that our current life is "evanescent," a small moment when compared to infinity.[53]

Reincarnation is the continuous cycle of rebirth. The lineage of Dalai Lamas began more than 600 years ago, yet there are many more bodhisattvas, those enlightened beings believed to forgo *nirvana* in order to be reborn for the benefit of others. The final goal of Buddhism is a transcendent state in which there is no suffering, desire, or sense of self, and one is released from the effects of karma as well as the cycle of death and rebirth.

The 14th Dalai Lama—Jetsun Jamphel Ngawang Losang Yeshe Tenzin Gyatso, known to many Tibetans as "the Presence"—has served longer than Queen Elizabeth. He took the throne at the age of 5. As Tibetans' leading spiritual figure, he is believed to be the reincarnation of Chenrezig (Avalokiteshvara), the Buddha of Compassion and patron saint of Tibet. The Dalai Lama refers to his own death as "a change of clothing." As a Buddhist, he says he visualizes death every day. He has mused that he might be reincarnated as a woman.

The second-most-important figure in Tibetan Buddhism is the Panchen Lama, the reincarnation of Amitabha, the Buddha of Boundless Light. Both the Dalai Lama and the Panchen Lama are seen as reincarnations of their predecessors. Traditionally, each acts as a mentor to the other and plays a key role in identifying the other's reincarnation.

As detailed on his website, the 14th Dalai Lama has listed the following as his principal commitments:

1. Encouraging people to be happy. He advocates for warm-heartedness, compassion, forgiveness, tolerance, contentment, and self-discipline. He is rooted in the conviction that we are all the same—we want happiness and do not want suffering.

2. Encouraging harmony among the world's religions. The world's major religions all have the potential for creating good human beings, so it is important that they respect one another.

3. Preserving the Tibetan language and culture, including Tibet's natural environment. He knows he is the focus of the Tibetan people's hope and trust.

4. Reviving awareness of the value of ancient Indian knowledge. He feels that a combination of ancient and modern modes of knowing can provide a more ethically grounded way to exist in contemporary society.[54]

KARMA, OR THE LAW OF CAUSE AND EFFECT

Since Buddhists believe in reincarnation or rebirth, karma plays a role. Each action we take leads to a new existence after death, an endless cycle called *samsara* that is considered unsatisfactory and painful. The cycle stops only if we achieve liberation through insight, awareness, and an ending of craving.

While modern society may view karma as "what goes around comes around," the Buddhist interpretation of karma refers to the "good" or "bad" actions a person takes during her lifetime. Good actions can be positive acts (generosity, righteousness, meditation) or simply the absence of bad actions, all of which can bring happiness in the long run. In contrast, bad actions (such as lying, stealing, or killing) can bring unhappiness.

Five conditions determine the karmic weight of one's actions:

1. Frequent, repetitive action

2. Determined, intentional action

3. Action performed without regret

4. Action against extraordinary persons

5. Action toward those who have helped one in the past

There is also neutral karma, which comes from acts such as breathing, eating, or sleeping. Neutral karma carries no benefits or costs.[55]

THE SIX REALMS OF REBIRTH

According to Buddhist philosophy, there are six separate planes or *gati* (realms) into which any living being can be reborn—three of them fortunate and three unfortunate:

- Deva (gods)
- Asura (demigods)
- Manusya (humans)
- Tiryak (animals)
- Preta (ghosts)
- Naraka (residents of hell)[56]

Those with positive karma (*kushala*) are reborn into one of the fortunate planes: the realms of demigods, gods, and humans. But while demigods and gods enjoy endless gratification, they also suffer unceasing jealousy and envy. Those with bad karma (*akushala*) become inhabitants of the three unfortunate realms: animals, ghosts, and hell, where they experience untold suffering.

The human realm is actually considered the highest realm of rebirth. It's notable that the suffering that happens in the realm of man is also far less than what occurs in "the three unfortunate realms."

What may be the most important part of the realm of man is a unique aspect unavailable in the other five: the opportunity to achieve enlightenment, or nirvana. To Buddhists, to be born human is a precious chance at spiritual bliss—a privilege that should not be forsaken.

BUDDHIST PRINCIPLES

Because of its myriad philosophies and interpretations, Buddhism tends to be a tolerant and evolving tradition that doesn't acknowledge a supreme god or deity. Historically, Buddhism has developed various schools and teachings in order to meet the needs and abilities of different peoples. Many meditative techniques have been perfected to help us clarify and cope with life's problems, and to get in touch with the profound aspects of our bodies and minds.

In Tibet specifically, Nyingma masters have been inclusive of different lifestyles. According to Tarthang Tulku, Head Lama of the Tibetan Nyingma Meditation Center in Berkeley, California, it's important to create adaptable and open-minded practices to help people establish a path of growth that's right for them, so we can all find inner peace in the midst of a troubled world. Given Buddhism's underpinning as a "way of life," Buddhists believe that you can practice in your home, in a temple, or wherever you are. This approach is taken throughout this book—apply what works for you, your lifestyle, and your body type, and leave the rest. What resonates with you now may not resonate with you in the future, and vice versa.

Tulku shares that the path to enlightenment is attained by using "morality, meditation, and wisdom." One of the first and most basic Buddhist principles, he says, is confronting life directly—taking time for genuine self-reflection with as open a mind and heart as possible.[57] The starting point of this entire journey is being honest with ourselves. Meditation, in addition to the other practices described throughout this book, can be a path toward awakening your inner truth.

THE THREE JEWELS

Buddhists believe there are three different expressions of the awakened mind: *buddha*, *dharma*, and *sangha*. Because these form an essential element of the Buddhist path, they are known as "the three jewels." As explained in the *Lion's Roar* magazine:

1. Buddha. The term "jewel of Buddha" refers to all teachers and guides who show us the "middle way," a way of existing between two extremes. The historical Buddha was a human being who lived more than 2,500 years ago and abandoned his life of wealth after seeing immense poverty.

2. Dharma. Known as "The Teachings," the Sanskrit word *dharma* denotes basic law or truths. It is also used to refer to the body of Buddhist teachings.

3. Sangha. While the Sanskrit term *sangha* originally referred to monastics (monks and nuns), in the Western world it has come to mean the community of Buddhist practitioners, or simply a Buddhist group to which individuals belong. The sangha is seen as

the repository of learning and spirituality for society; the 14th Dalai Lama believes that a happy life is dependent on the community.[58]

THE FOUR NOBLE TRUTHS

At the core of Buddha's most important teachings are the Four Noble Truths, which explain the nature and cause of suffering and the way to enlightenment. These are the Four Noble Truths:

1. The truth of suffering

2. The truth of the cause of suffering

3. The truth of the end of suffering

4. The truth of the path that leads to the end of suffering

Together, these explain both why humans hurt and how we can overcome suffering. The notion of suffering is not meant to portray a negative world view but rather offers a pragmatic perspective to help us deal with—and heal—the world as it is.

> *"It's an exaggeration and a misunderstanding of what the Buddha said to think that everything is suffering—the Buddha said there is suffering, but he didn't say that's all there is. There are causes that bring about suffering, and it's possible to arrive at a state of absence of these causes. There is always something. But we can handle suffering and happiness in an artful way."*
>
> *—Tarthang Tulku, Head Lama of the Nyingma Institute in Berkeley, California[59]*

THE NOBLE EIGHTFOLD PATH

The Buddha taught his followers that the end of suffering, as described in the Four Noble Truths, could be achieved by following an Eightfold Path. The following steps in this path (taken in any order) teach ethical conduct, mental discipline, and wisdom:

1. Right understanding

2. Right thought

3. Right speech

4. Right action

5. Right livelihood

6. Right effort

7. Right mindfulness

8. Right concentration

This Eightfold Path is divided into three themes: good moral conduct (understanding, thought, speech); meditation and mental development (action, livelihood, effort); and wisdom or insight (mindfulness, concentration).[60]

TIBETAN WATER-OFFERING BOWLS

The most common offerings at Tibetan Buddhist shrines are made with seven water-offering bowls, a ritual called *yonchap*. As with many Eastern spiritual traditions, these small bowls often contain symbolic offerings such as flowers, food, or incense. The point is to cultivate generosity by giving with an open and pure heart, with no attachment or expectation of receiving anything in return. Water is used because it's plentiful and free, therefore easy to give. The seven bowls represent the seven aspects of prayer:

- Prostrating (placing one's body in a reverential position, such as bowing or kneeling)

- Making offerings to the Buddhas or bodhisattvas

- Confessing our wrongs

- Celebrating our good qualities and those of others

- Requesting the Buddhas to remain in this world; bodhisattvas are beings who've chosen to forgo enlightenment to help other sentient beings

- Asking the Buddhas to teach others

- Devoting ourselves to service, so that we can help everyone enjoy happiness and live with integrity

Chapter 6

MORE PRACTICES FOR REJUVENATION

"We respond to light like plants, continuously moving toward greater alignment with the light and the consciousness that underlies it, while interacting with the qualities and quantities of light that best support our physical, emotional, and spiritual development. We are creatures of light."

— Jacob Liberman, *Luminous Life*[61]

In his book *Luminous Life: How the Science of Light Unlocks the Art of Living*, Dr. Jacob Israel Liberman explores the connection between light, vision, and consciousness at the intersection of science with spirituality, quantum physics with mysticism, and neuroscience with Eastern philosophy. Much like the Tibetan Buddhist belief that we live in a relational universe where everything is intimately connected, Liberman says that because we are each a cell within the organism called "the universe," we're designed to infinitely communicate and cooperate with one another.

The more *you* heal and thrive, therefore, the more you help the world to do the same. It's fascinating to see spiritual thinkers and quantum physicists describe God and light in the same ways. Light is the foundation of everything that exists—omnipotent, omniscient, and omnipresent. As Liberman notes, everything we experience in life as matter is the formed expression of a formless essence called light, and human beings are holographic focal points of that light. Or, as American theoretical physicist David Bohm has said, "All matter is frozen light."[62]

When we embrace all that life and light have to offer, we experience "presence." When we allow the light within us to merge with the light that guides us, we can experience the oneness described in Tibetan Buddhism—and through moments of meditation, presence can even find us.

Many of us have been trained to believe that disease is contagious, yet what if we learn to believe that wellness is even more contagious?

MORE ABOUT MINDFULNESS

Earlier in this book we explored the Tibetan Buddhist belief that to be born human is a rare privilege, and therefore it's important to have gratitude for our lives and to take advantage of the opportunity we have been given. Yet being human is hard.

It's hard to experience love and loss, joy and disappointment, connection and fracturing. It's hard to be in a body that can experience pleasure as much as pain. And it's hard to know that everything we are attached to is perpetually changing—and, ultimately, fleeting.

However, there's a flip side. If you were brought two bouquets of flowers, one completely made of plastic and the other a fresh bunch of lilies, which one would seem more beautiful? Most likely, the fresh bouquet. But, why? Because in general, we understand that the fresh flowers will die—their beauty is fleeting. It's precisely this temporal nature that makes the flowers so special.

Similarly, this is why mindfulness can be so incredibly powerful. We become more present in our daily lives and uncover how precious each moment can be, because we know that it won't last forever. The mindfulness practices explored in this chapter will enable you to become deeply aware of what you're sensing and feeling *in the moment* without interpretation or judgment, creating an opportunity to be *with* whatever it is that you're going through.

There's a common misperception that meditating or practicing mindfulness will instantly lead to a sense of inner peace and bliss. Yet becoming fully present can be extremely challenging, because as we allow for everything—the entire spectrum of emotions and experiences—we are brought to reflect on hard moments and truths we may have been trying to push away. Almost all spiritual disciplines practice some form of meditation, because this path offers a process of seeking truth or understanding, of discovering the nature of existence and the human mind, of knowing yourself more deeply. Mindfulness requires a sense of courageous honesty. We stop running. Instead, we look deeply into ourselves and the situation we're in right now.

Meditation can generate three types of energy:

- ❀ Mindfulness
- ❀ Concentration
- ❀ Insight

These three energies give us the power to nourish happiness and take care of ourselves, to discover who we truly are in whatever we're presently experiencing, good or bad, challenging or easy, peaceful or turbulent.

While specific practices are suggested here for mind, body, and spirit, be sure to make your practice your own. Explore what you need in the present moment and whatever works best for the development of stillness and concentration right now. Remember, this is *your* journey home.

SIMPLE PRACTICES FOR THE MIND

Whether we're aware of it or not, we're constantly trying to protect our egos and self-images. This is one of the hardest of human behavioral habits to let go of. American sociologist Charles Horton Cooley reflected upon the complexity of one's personal identity with this statement: "I am not who you think I am; I am not who I think I am; I am who I think you think I am."[63]

As shared by Tarthang Tulku, Head Lama of the Nyingma Institute in Berkeley, California, "We often live as if we're in a dream. We're dragged into the past or pulled into the future. We're bound by our sorrow, agitation, and fear. We hold on to our anger, which blocks communication. 'Liberation' means transforming and transcending these conditions in order to be fully awake, at ease, peaceful, joyful and fresh. We practice stopping and observing deeply in order to arrive at liberation. When we live in this way, our life is worth living, and we become a source of joy to our family and to everyone around us."[64]

Buddhist teachers throughout millennia have shared great compassion for human beings, because they see how exhausted we are made by our constant grasping. By becoming more disciplined, taking responsibility for ourselves, and making the big or small choices to lean in toward love rather than away from it, we can experience a sense of inner freedom, even in the most challenging of circumstances.

When you become more aware of the mind, you can begin to see that you may not be responsible for your first thought. That can often be a patterned reaction to what's happening in the moment. But you *are* responsible for the next one. What will your next thought be?

> *"We weigh just 100 or 200 pounds and stand only five or six feet high, yet most of our problems are in our heads, which are only eight inches wide—and this we find hard to take care!"*
>
> —*Tarthang Tulku, Head Lama of the Nyingma Institute*[65]

MORE ABOUT THE MIND

Twenty quadrillion bits of information move around in our brain *every second*!

The human brain has two very different processing systems. The first responds quickly, instinctually, and unconsciously, controlled by the right hemisphere, the ancient limbic or "reptilian" parts of our brain. The second responds slowly, logically, and consciously, and it is controlled by the left hemisphere and the neocortex.[66]

If you're wondering about intuition, that resides in the first system. Researchers have found that intuition can provide us with immediate answers—usually correct—long before the second system even gets started.

There are three levels of human consciousness:

- *Conscious*: defines our thoughts, actions, and awareness
- *Subconscious*: the reactions
- *Unconscious*: the deep recesses of our past, including memories.[67]

In the *conscious* mind, we can readily acknowledge feelings and thoughts, whereas the *unconscious* is a process that happens automatically and stores all our repressed thoughts and feelings. The *subconscious*, however, is a secondary mind system that regulates just about everything in our life. It's the part of the mind that isn't in focal awareness at the moment—a barrier our mind makes to deal with the constant barrage of information received through our senses.

Like an iceberg, our thoughts are mostly beneath the surface. Researchers have estimated that about 10 percent of our thoughts are conscious (some experts even reduce this by half), 50 to 60 percent subconscious, and 30 to 40 percent unconscious. Our conscious mind *thinks* it knows, while the unconscious mind *knows*, without knowing that it knows. The journal of *Behavioral and Brain Sciences* published a study led by associate professor of neuroscience Ezequiel Morsella of San Francisco State University; the study concluded that nearly all the brain's work is conducted at the unconscious level.[68]

As Liberman asks in *Luminous Life*, since the conscious mind of the ego and the unconscious mind of infinite potential are both aspects of our totality, why do we identify with the limited view of the conscious mind rather than the unlimited view of the unconscious?[69]

With such complexity in our minds, it's easy to get frustrated with our thoughts or behaviors. Yet in everything from physics to chemistry to human interactions, these "disruptions" often are the catalysts that bring change. And as Tibetan Buddhism affirms, the one constant in life is change or impermanence.

> *"Electrons jump to a higher orbit when they are perturbed. Chemical reactions occur when homeostasis or stability is disturbed. And, human beings often transform themselves when they are stressed. We cannot even wash our clothes without agitation."*
>
> —*Joseph Liberman*, Luminous Light[70]

WHERE IS YOUR ATTENTION GOING?

You may have heard the saying "Where attention goes, energy flows." Thinking feeds the mind and starves the body. Breathing calms the mind, inspires, and feeds life into the body.

Try taking a deep breath right now.

Sometimes it's helpful to just forget our problems for a short time. By doing so, we can see that we've gotten caught up in the energy of worrying, anxiety, or stress, that we've narrowed our perspective—thereby preventing us from constructively dealing with our difficulties.

What would happen if you broke up this pattern? How would it feel to be, do, say, or feel the *opposite* of what you would normally do?

Recognize the power of your emotions and accept responsibility for them by taking a light and positive attitude about yourself. This moment of self-compassion and joy can alleviate states of hopelessness, loneliness, and despair.

MANTRAM AND MANTRA IN "THE LOST CHAPTER"

The discovery of a lost 1946 edition of Kelder's *The Eye of Revelation* added two sections specifically about the mind, focused on what the author called Mantram Mind Magic:

- "Mantram Mind Magic" suggests a new way of communicating directly with your subconscious to seed affirmations.

⚜ "Magic Qualities of Aum" reveals how to combine affirmations with the age-old practice of chanting *aum* (see page 105).

There's a slight difference between the words "mantra" and "mantram." Both come from a Sanskrit word meaning "instrument of thought," but a mantram is vocalized while a mantra is silent.

Mantram Mind Magic is designed to help you realize that anything in your physical reality is first created in your mind. In other words, whether you realize it or not, you create and shape your life with your thoughts. All things that are now part of your physical reality were first created in your mind via your thoughts. Therefore, because a mantram is an *instrument of thought*, you can use it to help shape your life the way you want it to be.

According to neuroscience expert Joe Dispenza, DC, author of *Evolve Your Brain: The Science of Changing Your Mind*, "I think one of my greatest realizations in my own journey was just because you have a thought, that doesn't necessarily mean it's true. So if you think 60 to 70,000 thoughts in one day, and we do, and 90 percent of those thoughts are the same thoughts as the day before, and you believe that your thoughts have something to do with your destiny, your life's not going to change very much because the same thought leads to the same choice, the same choice leads to the same behavior, the same behavior creates the same experience, and the same experience produces the same emotion. And so then the act of becoming conscious of this process, to begin to become more aware of how you think, how you act, and how you feel is called metacognition."[71]

To use mantrams to your advantage, it's helpful to understand how the mind works. Modern-day science talks a lot about the subconscious, but instead of "subconsciousness," the lamas use a word that could be translated as "superconsciousness"—a consciousness of a higher order. The job of your superconscious mind is to take thought, which is pure energy, and give it physical shape in the material world.

Susan Moran explains in *Yoga Journal* that the word "mantra" comes from the Sanskrit words *manas* (mind) and *tra* (tool). Therefore, mantra can be translated as "a tool for the mind." A mantra can be chanted, whispered, or silently recited. As Moran writes, "Neuroscientists...are beginning to quantify and confirm some of the health benefits of this ancient practice, such as its ability to free your mind of chatter and calm your nervous system." And Herbert Benson, founder of the Benson-Henry Institute for Mind Body Medicine at Massachusetts General Hospital, has found through his research that no matter what word or phrase a person repeats, it can produce relaxation to help cope with stress.[72]

Kelder says that your superconscious is a willing and eager "servant" that you can command. When you think a thought, you issue a command. Your "servant" obeys by manifesting the thought into your physical reality, where it becomes the objects and events of your life.

Ultimately, your physical reality is a mirror of what you're thinking—which means that if you change your thought patterns, you can change your life! Every thought, idea, and belief materializes into a chemical messenger that is simultaneously experienced by every cell of the body. In 1985, Dr. Candace Pert showed that there are mechanisms through which the emotions, originating in the limbic system, affect the immune system, creating a deeply interdependent feedback loop. These findings indicate that every state of mind manifests as neuropeptides, neurotransmitters, hormones, and pheromones. This has become the foundation of mind-body medicine, or psychoneuroimmunology.[73]

At times our thoughts and our behaviors may be at odds with one another. In one breath we say, "I want to be happy," but in the very next breath we focus on everything that brings us unhappiness and even complain about this to the people in our lives—things like a stressful job, bills or debt, discomfort in our bodies, feeling overwhelmed with too much to do, and the list goes on. Your goal is contentment, but your thoughts are working overtime to create just the opposite feeling. What can you do? You can use a mantram.

A MAGIC MIND-SHIFT EXERCISE

A mantram can help you sync your thought patterns and bring them into alignment with your highest and greatest desires.

1. Start by clearly identifying what you'd like to manifest in your life. Take a moment to write down—actually using a pen and paper—a list of the things you desire most. Do this in the form of a stream of consciousness, not thinking too much about what you "should" or "shouldn't" ask for. Simply include everything that comes to mind.

2. Now reflect upon your list. Ask yourself what's at the core of each "want." For example, let's say you wrote that you want a better job. What would be the rewards of having a better job? A greater sense of fulfillment? Shining a bright light on your talents? More compensation and a greater sense of security? Or perhaps you're looking to connect with a great team of colleagues. Whatever it is, get specific about how you want to *feel*.

The rewards you list should be feelings, as material possessions will not come with us at the end of life.

3. Review your list of desires and the feelings you want to have. As you read each item, choose two or three words or phrases that summarize the whole list. If you take a deep breath and settle into a feeling of calm, you might see that there are seemingly different wants that are aimed at a common goal. Separate your desires into two or three groups and find a word or phrase that encapsulates each group. For instance, let's say that you wrote down that you want to buy a new car, to buy a house, and to be able to go out to eat whenever you'd like. At the core of these is the idea of *abundance* and *prosperity*.

4. When you have your keywords, put them all together and state a brief positive command. Yes, it's okay to ask the universe *firmly* for what you want and to say that you want it *right now*. For example, you might say, "I demand happiness, power, and abundance right now." That's it! When your command—or your mantram—is spoken aloud, plainly and clearly, it becomes a device you can use to stimulate your superconscious mind into action. Using "right now" emphasizes to your superconscious

mind that it needs to get busy immediately manifesting your desires.

Both Kelder and Bradford would encourage you to be bold and speak with conviction, "speak as if you are commanding a magic genie who will bring you whatever you desire. Once you have spoken your mantram aloud with unwavering conviction and resolve, you've done all that's needed."[74]

Speak your mantram just before going to bed at night and right when you wake up in the morning. Make it a habit to repeat it at regular intervals throughout the day. It can be especially impactful to look at your reflection in a mirror, gazing straight into your own eyes, and repeat your mantram with firm confidence.

As you go about your day, become aware of any negative thoughts or words that send conflicting messages to your superconscious mind. When you spot one, take a deep breath, say "cancel," and then speak your mantram again.

You might sometimes be around other people and find it awkward to utter a keyword or phrase aloud. That's when a mantra—the silent version—comes into play. You can repeat your mantram inwardly and silently, contemplating the meaning of your words.

There's one important catch: when you command your superconscious mind to go to work, you must focus only on the end result that you desire. Never try to dictate *how* the superconsciousness will accomplish its magic for you. It's not your job to worry about the "how," only the "what" of your wishes. Your superconscious mind is far more clever and resourceful than your conscious mind; it knows that there are innumerable ways to achieve what you want. If *you* try to figure it out, you'll only limit its options and restrict how the magic will unfold.

It might be helpful to know that your superconscious mind doesn't judge your thoughts before responding to them. It doesn't differentiate between joy or sorrow, pain or pleasure. Its job is to transform all thought patterns into matter. Said another way, the universe wants only to make you happy, and it does this by pursuing the things you put the most energy into. If you're constantly focused on challenges in your life, the universe translates that as what you're seeking more of. And if you're focused on gratitude, appreciation, love, and abundance, that's where it goes to work for you.

As you grow and change, let your mantram grow and change with you. Let it be in words that *you* would use, so that it sounds believable to your heart and your mind. There's one exception, and that is with the word *om* or *aum*, as explained below. The power of this word lies in its tonal vibration. Kelder sometimes called this "Rite Number Seven."

HOW TO PRACTICE "AUM," OR "RITE NUMBER SEVEN"

In yoga, when the word *aum* is intoned correctly, the vibratory frequency has a powerful stimulating effect on the pineal gland, which is related to the seventh and highest vortex, focused on higher consciousness. You may already have practiced chanting "aum" or "om" in yoga classes you've taken. What did you notice when you did that?

For at least a month before you begin this Rite, drink an increased amount of water each day. Water not only helps to cleanse your body of wastes and impurities, but it's also a conductor of electrical current and sound vibration.

1. To begin, stand, sit in a comfortable seat, or lie on your back on the floor on a mat or a rug with nothing beneath your head. Relax completely with your spine straight and your chin up, ensuring that your vocal cords are not constricted.

2. Draw the "au" sound—pronounced "ah"—out through your mouth for about five seconds. Then close your mouth (not suddenly) and hum the "m" sound out through your nose for 10 seconds. Don't fill your lungs to bursting, but simply take in enough air to do the vibration for 15 seconds (five seconds through the mouth, 10 seconds through the nose) without being completely out of breath.

3. After a breath or two, do the "au-mmmmmmm" sound again. Three or four times in succession is a great start, but stop right away if you begin to feel dizzy.

4. Wait an hour or so and then perform the sound again several times. At first, don't do so more than 10 times, even if you feel no dizziness. For a beginner, too much pineal stimulation is not a positive.

5. While you repeat your affirmation mentally in the mantra Rite and repeat your affirmation vocally for the mantram, this one is

a combination of both. While you are vocalizing the "ah" in aum, hold your mind quiet; while intoning the "m," repeat whatever affirmation you're focusing on mentally several times.

HOW TO CALM YOUR MIND? STOP RUNNING

According to psychologist and author Rollo May, "One does not become fully human painlessly."[75] The good news? You've made it through every single one of the hardest moments of your life so far.

Many of us are used to running, especially from pain. We think happiness and well-being aren't possible in the present. We're comparing our insides to someone else's outsides, our lowlights to someone else's highlight reel, and we experience suffering as a result.

Meditation has one key aspect: *stopping*. We are running throughout our whole life, chasing after some idea of happiness. Status, financial success, relationship—whatever "it" is for us. Stopping means to stop our running, our forgetfulness of who we truly are, our being caught in the past or the future. When we stop, we arrive in the present moment, where real life is available. In this present moment, as you are reading this, you are safe. You are whole. You contain the entire universe within you. In the present moment, we have the power to calm our bodies and emotions. We can stop chasing and let everything that we want catch up with us. We can start arriving at everything we've worked so hard to create.

If you can stop, pause, and arrive in the here and now, you can see that there's more than enough for you to be happy, even if there are a few things in the present that aren't your favorites. There are still plenty of conditions for which to be grateful. Often when we compare ourselves to others, we find that we have "less than"—yet how often do we compare ourselves to someone who has less than us? How often are we giving versus grasping?

BECOME MORE PRESENT, MORE SATISFIED

By focusing on the past or the future, we're never fully present, and therefore we're never truly satisfied. We're constantly expecting that in the future there will be something greater, better, more fulfilling—but because we keep pushing away the present moment, we never actually arrive at that moment. Our whole lives consist of endless preparations, without any of the payoff we're looking for.

If that sounds like you, you're not alone! Most of us don't know how to begin accepting each present moment. We say we want to enjoy life and experience pleasure, but our minds keep projecting satisfaction into the future rather than the now. How can we accomplish anything in the present moment if our minds are constantly oriented toward some future goal? Yes, planning for the future is indeed helpful. The Tibetan Buddhist approach is not to nix that tendency; we simply need to learn how to live more fully in the here and now.

Here's the ironic truth: living more fully in the present naturally leads us into the future. Another way to say this is that we don't need to be too concerned with the future, since the present will lead us there no matter what we do. What's more, the future we want changes according to how we live in the present. The more confident we become with the actions and meaning of our daily lives, the more balanced and harmonious our future lives can become.

If we can develop the practice of finding more fulfillment, joy, and calm *in the now*, then as the future arrives we're already enjoying the result we've been working so hard to attain. When we open ourselves to our present experiences, we are able to realize that we can enjoy our lives *right now*!

PRESENT MOMENT AWARENESS MEDITATION

It's natural for the mind to "think." Sometimes giving it something to think *about* can help you achieve a clearer, calmer mind.

Have you felt that your awareness of the present moment is dull or unclear, that it feels like something is going on in the shadows behind your consciousness, or that you're losing time and energy? Here's a practice to help you to become more present. By shifting your attention to your senses and focusing deeply on your breath, you can automatically drop into the present moment:

SOUNDS. What sounds do you notice around you? From traffic to nearby voices or music to birds chirping and wind rustling, simply allow the sounds to wash over you. Say aloud, "I am aware of this present moment."

SENSATIONS. Where are you sitting? Where are you standing? What do your clothes feel like against your skin? Do you have any tingling, tension, or tightness in your body? Without judgment, simply observe what you are feeling in your body. Say aloud, "I am aware of this present moment."

THOUGHTS. Mindfulness is observing without judgment, without the need for change, without becoming attached. Whatever thoughts arise, simply observe them, label them, and let them go. If it helps, you can say "Noting" (to yourself or aloud) to note that you are having a thought. Say aloud, "I am aware of this present moment."

BREATHING. The more fully you can bring your attention to your inhalation and exhalation, the more you can drop into the present moment. Notice where you feel your breath in your body. Observe its quality, whether it is full or shallow. Breathe naturally and deeply. Once again say aloud, "I am aware of this present moment."

LEARN TO EMBRACE CHANGE

When we realize that everything in our lives is always changing— just as the universe is ever expanding—we can be *with* our life situations by not becoming attached to or dragged down by them.

In parenting, there's a common saying: "This too shall pass." From the most wonderfully poignant moments to the meltdowns and tantrums, everything is impermanent. We can appreciate the beautiful moments more, knowing they will pass; we can suffer less in the difficult times, knowing this too shall pass.

We struggle when we want things that we know will cause us pain or frustration. Yet such habit patterns can be hard to break; even when we try, obstacles seem to appear. Our tendencies push us to repeat the same destructive patterns; our self-identity is so strong that we don't want to lose our sense of control over ourselves, our environment, or even other people.

Tibetan Buddhist teachers point out that most of us look upon death as a loss rather than an opportunity. We're afraid of losing our egos and reluctant to give up our attachments and habit patterns, because we often don't know who we are without them. But until we let go of the attachment to what we believe is our personality, it's difficult to see these life patterns, let alone change them.

RELAX INTO A NEW KNOWING

You don't need to set aside a special time to relax, and you don't need any special equipment. You don't even need more than five minutes. You simply need one cycle of breath.

Right now? This is a good time to begin.

Zen master and Vietnamese monk Thich Nhat Hanh says that as humans, we have lost confidence in our bodies' knowing what to do. If we have time alone with ourselves, we panic and try to do many different things.[76] Mindful breathing helps us relearn the art of resting. Mindful breathing is like telling yourself, "Don't worry, I'll take good care of you; just relax."

> Take a deep breath in. Breathe a deep breath out. In the spaciousness that you create with that breath, you have an opportunity to examine your tendency, your pattern, your behavior. Then, in the next cycle of breath, you can choose differently.
>
> Breathe in. Breathe out.

SIMPLE PRACTICES FOR THE BODY

In modern life, we tend to think that our bodies belong to us, that we can do anything we want to them. Yet our bodies are not only ours. Our bodies belong to the earth, to our parents and our ancestors, and to future generations, society, and all other living beings.

We also tend to think of the body as only a physical entity made up of skin, bones, muscles, and internal organs. It may be hard to understand that your body is like "space," since the physical structure seems solid. But the space outside the body and the space within it are not separate.

Another way to look at this is that "you're mostly a series of electron clouds, all bound together by the same quantum rules that govern the entire universe," as astrophysicist Ethan Siegel explains. [77] The more you relax, the more you can feel internal and external space become one. This feeling of oneness is important, because it's one way we can begin to connect to the healing energy within and around us.

BE BEAUTIFUL, BE YOURSELF BODY SCAN

If you can accept your body, then you have a chance to see your body as home. But in a world that often focuses on physical appearance, it can be difficult to feel comfortable with our physical selves—and this doesn't even take into consideration the aches and pains we may feel when we're experiencing any ailments. If you don't accept your body as well as your mind, you can't be at home with yourself.

Use the following body scan practice as an opportunity to connect with yourself without judgment—to learn to accept yourself just as you are in this moment. This practice takes only a few minutes. You can do it sitting or lying down.

1. To begin, bring all of your awareness to the top of your head.

2. Now start to feel that awareness cascade down your body toward your toes.

3. Choose one area of your body that is calling for your attention. Focus on your breath, and on your next inhalation say, "Inhaling, I am aware of my...," completing the sentence with that body part.

4. As you exhale, say, "Exhaling, I smile to my...," again naming the body part.

5. Once or twice each day, pick at least one part of your body to focus on, and practice relaxing into gratitude.

In traditional Tibetan medicine, a person's entire system is naturally self-sufficient. The cure for sickness is within each of us, because the natural state is balance or homeostasis. Whatever we need is uniquely there.

The prescription is there; the remedy is there. Yet these days most of us depend on external or artificial means to stay healthy and free from pain. If we can bring ourselves back into balance so that our life-force energy is flowing smoothly, our bodies and minds have the resources to protect themselves. We can open ourselves to positive energies around us and channel them throughout the body.

Once we have control of these subtle energies, we can distribute that control to the physical body, the emotional body, and the psychic body. In other words, we have the opportunity to re-create our bodies through positive energy. In fact, science has shown that we make a new skeleton every three months and a new layer of skin every month, so we do indeed have the ability to refine and transform our bodies into healthy, clear, and open channels.

INCREDIBLE FACTS ABOUT YOUR BODY

Here are a few remarkable things you might not know about the human body, as pointed out on the website MarthaStewart. com:[78]

🏵 In a single hour, your heart produces enough energy to raise a ton of steel three feet off the ground.

🏵 The human heart will beat approximately three billion times during an average person's lifetime.

- The human eye can distinguish up to a million different colors and take in more information than the largest telescope known to man.
- When we touch something, the signal travels through the nerves to our brain at a speed of 124 mph.
- The human liver is responsible for more than 500 distinct body processes. In fact, it's so important that if a person has to have up to two-thirds of their liver removed, it'll grow back to its original size in as little as four weeks.
- The average person takes 23,000 breaths in a day.

With the Tibetan Buddhist belief that we are the caretakers of our bodies rather than their owners, we can approach the practice of eating—and what we choose to eat—with mindfulness.

You can eat in a way that allows you to be aware that each bite is deepening your connection to the planet. Barley, for instance, takes 90 days from seed to harvest. While we often eat in a rush from one thing to the next, the numerable steps it takes for food to arrive at your plate—and the many people and elements of the planet it requires to create that sustenance—is remarkable in and of itself.

When we can slow down and really enjoy our food, life takes on a much deeper quality. In Waldorf schools throughout America, the tradition is for young children to eat in silence and reverence, appreciating the hard and loving work that has gone into each bite of food.[79]

There's a saying in Buddhist philosophies: "Chew your food, not your worries." Instead of thinking of the past, the future, a worry or anxiety, relationships or work, you can simply become more present as you chew your food. When you eat this way, not only will you feel physically nourished, but you'll also feel spiritually nourished. The way you eat influences everything else that you will do during the day.

After eating and before rushing on to the next thing, spend a moment being grateful for the food you have eaten and for your body processing the nutrients and removing the toxins.

Eating can become an important time for meditation, a chance to receive the many gifts of the earth that you would not otherwise benefit from if your mind were elsewhere. From setting the table to putting down the phone to appreciating the company around you, every moment can become more mindful by simply focusing on your breath.

After sitting and engaging your parasympathetic nervous system ("rest and digest") as opposed to your sympathetic nervous system ("fight or flight"), you need only a second or two to recognize that the whole universe, the earth and the sky, has collaborated to bring this meal to you. Every morsel of food, every moment of eating, has mindfulness in it.

By having this deference, this understanding of what a luxury it is to be able to be nourished, we can become more mindful of how to create sustainability and sustenance for all.

PRACTICE A TEA MEDITATION

As you're preparing your tea, from boiling the water to choosing the leaves, you can begin to clear your mind. Choosing a quality organic loose-leaf tea can create a sense of ceremony, although a tea bag is wonderful, too. If you can, use filtered water.

● Find a space to enjoy your tea, possibly the same place where you practice the Five Tibetan Rites. Before entering this area, consider trying to leave behind anything that you'd like to release.

● Take time to appreciate the tea. Where did it come from? Can you imagine where the leaves were grown? Who cultivated it for you? Breathe in and acknowledge all the steps it took to bring this tea to your lips. Give thanks.

● Drink the tea and take in the subtle scents, the tastes, the way you feel as it moves past your lips, down your throat, into your body. This can be seen as a moment of culmination. Be present with each unfolding moment.

● Practice for as long as you wish, at any time of day. Even cleaning up afterward can become a ritual, as you express thanks to yourself for showing up in this present moment.

TIBETAN RITES FOOD RECOMMENDATIONS

If you'd like to follow traditional eating habits for the Five Tibetan Rites, Kelder observes in *The Eye of Revelation* that different types of food require different digestive processes in the stomach. If a starch such as a bread is eaten together with a protein such as meat, each interferes with the digestion of the other. The end result, says Kelder, is that neither the bread nor the meat is fully digested; a good part of the food's nutritional value is lost; bloating and physical distress occur; and valuable energy, which could be put to a better use, is depleted in the process.[80]

He also suggests eating slowly. Chewing is the first important step in preparing food to be assimilated by the body. Everything you eat should be thoroughly broken down in the mouth before it is digested in the stomach. If you gulp down food, as many do in our busy lifestyles, you'll bypass this vital step. The more completely a food is chewed, the more nourishing it will be. If you thoroughly chew your food, the amount you eat can be reduced—often by half.

To keep things simple, here's a summary of Kelder's suggestions:

- ❀ The right foods, the right combinations, the right amounts, and the right method of eating combine to produce wonderful results. Reduce to a minimum the variety of foods you eat in a single meal.

- ❀ Don't eat starch and meat at the same meal, though if you are strong and healthy, it need not cause you too much concern.

- ❀ If coffee bothers you, drink it without any milk or cream. If it still bothers you, eliminate it from your diet.

- ❀ Chew your food to a liquid consistency, and cut down on the total amount of food you eat.

- ❀ Eat raw egg yolks* once a day, every day, just before or just after meals—not during a meal.

- Eliminate or reduce fats of all kinds, especially lard. A small amount of butter is okay.

- Meat is acceptable in sensible and limited quantities, but eliminate pork completely.

- White sugar should be used sparingly; honey and natural sweets can be used in moderation instead.

- Eliminate alcohol completely if aiming to achieve a higher state of consciousness.

* The USDA recommends against the consumption of raw eggs, which can be contaminated with salmonella bacteria and can cause food poisoning.

WHERE FEELINGS LIVE IN YOUR BODY

Along with your physical and spiritual bodies, you have a "feelings body" that is filled with perceptions, thoughts, emotions, and deep consciousness. That's why movement practices are helpful for processing the emotions we experience in our lives.

Feelings can be positive, negative, or neutral, and they can seem to arise without any rational cause. Certain feelings are stronger in some areas of the body than in others, and they can vary in intensity at different times. (*BodyMind* by Ken Dychtwald is a great resource for learning where feelings can live in your body.)

Feelings can accumulate like dust and become so mixed together that it becomes difficult to sort through them. In the beginning, simply pinpointing the *area* and the *intensity* of your feelings will deepen awareness. Mindfulness helps to settle feelings in the body.

Mindfulness practices—such as breathing, walking, and eating mindfully—can not only nourish your body but can also help you courageously deal with your emotions, listen to and embrace your experiences, and recognize where in your body your feelings reside. This helps you find a sense of inner peace and an opportunity for healing.

The more you embrace your feelings and accept your experiences, even if they're unpleasant, the more you can help them to transform into something positive.

TRY A MOVING MEDITATION

When you walk in your neighborhood or a park, on a trail, or by the ocean, be aware of your breathing. Walking meditation is a way of integrating your mind with your body. If your mind is preoccupied with worries and anxieties, or if you're distracting yourself with a cell phone, you can't enjoy the present moment. You're missing out on life.

Use movement connected with breath to become more mindful and present. In the here and now, you can see how life has given you this present moment, the only moment in which life is available.

Take a deep breath as you walk in gratitude. With each step, connect to something or someone you can appreciate. Feel yourself as part of this planet. Feel the effortlessness of seeing the blue sky. You don't have to practice to enjoy it—you can just enjoy it. Each second, each minute of your life can be like this.

> Wherever you are, at any time, you have the capacity to enjoy the air, the presence of others, even the sensation of your breathing. You don't have to travel into the future to enjoy your breath or your blessings. You can be in touch with these things right now.

STRESS LESS FOR BETTER HEALTH

Stress accumulates in our bodies and affects all systems, including the musculoskeletal, respiratory, cardiovascular, endocrine, gastrointestinal, nervous, and reproductive systems. While our bodies are well equipped to handle stress in small doses, long-term or chronic stress can have serious effects on the body, as explained in detail on the American Psychological Association website.[81]

According to Jon Kabat-Zinn, founder of the Stress Reduction Clinic at the University of Massachusetts Medical School, a typical stress reaction—which most of us experience countless times a day—creates an avalanche of endless biochemical reactions. When left unchecked, these turn into illnesses, premature aging, and impaired cognitive function. Kabat-Zinn developed a mindfulness-based stress reduction program (MBSR) in 1979 that includes a mix of mindfulness meditation, body awareness practices, yoga, and exploring patterns of behavior, thinking, feeling, and action to better manage stress, anxiety, depression, and pain. In clinical studies over the last few decades, MBSR has been shown to contribute positively to pain management and improve quality of life.[82]

Neuroscience continues to show that many health issues are psychosomatic. In other words, a physical condition is caused or aggravated by a mental factor such as an internal conflict or stress. Depression, insomnia, digestive, or sexual disorders—these can all have a mental connection![83]

The good news is that we all have within us the resources to be healthy and balanced. It's simply a matter of directing and using our energies properly. This "direction" doesn't have to be forced. Instead, it's a natural process that begins to function when we learn to relax and use certain ways of breathing, feeling, and thinking that help adjust our inner balance and let our energies flow more freely.

The first step to take is to R-E-L-A-X. As a healing system, relaxation can be used to relieve our anxieties and frustrations, pressures that cause our energies to stagnate and cloud our ability to live to our fullest expression of self. The deeper we relax, the more we allow for our innate healing mechanisms to operate without creating more blocks, challenges, or obstacles.

Sometimes we think that we can relax only when we're lying down or when all the external conditions are just right. But we can actually relax at any moment, wherever we are and in the midst of whatever we're doing! We can do this by bringing awareness to the body and whatever feelings we're experiencing, such as noticing if we're clenching our jaw, how deep or shallow our breath is, whatever thoughts we're thinking. As with many Tibetan Buddhism practices, when we learn to relax body, breath, and mind, the body becomes healthier, the mind becomes clear, and awareness becomes balanced.

If your body is filled with tension and pain, you are not alone! The rigors of modern-day life can absolutely take a toll, especially if we don't build in time for rest. If you suppress or ignore whatever aches are calling for your attention, then the tension and pain tend to grow each day, preventing you from experiencing the happiness or contentment that is as natural to you as stress may have become. A ripple effect may begin to happen, where it becomes difficult to sleep, or to eat, and then the repercussions become exponential. That's why it's important to take daily small steps to reduce stress, as with the "massage" exercise described on page 124.

BRING PEACE WITH GENTLE MASSAGE

Focusing on your exhalations helps to bring a sense of calm and peace to your body as you begin to engage the parasympathetic ("rest and digest") nervous system that we'll explore more in the next section on the vagus nerve. Often, if you hear your stomach grumbling, you will know that you've relaxed to the point that your digestion can kick in—which is a great sign! When we're on alert, when we're stressed, we're in our sympathetic nervous system, so shifting attention to lengthening your exhales is one way to begin relaxing more deeply.

The quieter you become, the more energy you will be able to feel. In this way, you can experience your body as open space and live within that feeling.

1. Sit back on a chair and breathe deeply 10 to 15 times. Inhale very slowly and evenly through your nose. Hold your breath for just a moment. Now focus your attention on exhaling through your nose, extending the exhale. Feel the energy circulate through your bloodstream and gently observe your feelings.

2. As you breathe, relax your eyes and let your mouth fall open, loosening any tension in your jaw. Loosen all your muscles. Imagine sending your breath from the crown of your head to your feet, then as you exhale, sense your entire body from your toes to the top of your head. Wherever you feel tightness, tension, or pain, send your breath to those spaces.

3. Completely let go of stress and tension with every exhale.

4. Very gently and slowly massage your head, neck, chest, arms, legs, and feet so that you feel a warm flow of energy in each cell, helping your body to relax more deeply.

5. Your mind may be filled with chatter, judgments, worry, or anticipation. Simply observe these movements of your mind without following any particular thought. You can even say "noting" to yourself as you notice whatever comes up, without needing to make meaning of it.

6. Continue massaging anywhere on your body that is calling for your attention. Expand your feeling of relaxation energy as much as you can. Let your thinking become increasingly balanced as energy rises and circulates more freely throughout your entire system.

SUPPORT THE VAGUS NERVE
FOR HEALING ENERGY

The Five Tibetan Rites underscore that the power of self-healing is a reality—though many of us don't believe in it. In recent years the vagus nerve within the body has gotten well-deserved attention. The longest of the cranial nerves, it's the main component of the parasympathetic nervous system ("rest and digest") that oversees a vast array of crucial bodily functions, including mood control, immune response, digestion, and heart rate. Research shows that it may play a key part in treating chronic inflammation, as Jordan Rosenfeld reports in *Mental Floss* magazine, and this has launched a new field of bioelectronics treatment for serious, incurable diseases.[84] And the vagus nerve can be influenced by mindfulness and breathwork practices—see page 45 for breathwork practices.

HOW TO SUPPORT YOUR VAGUS NERVE

You have the power within you right now to support your own stress management, physical wellness, and mental health by supporting your vagus nerve. Here is a summary of ways to do so, as suggested by Jordan Fallis, founder of Optimal Living Dynamics.[85]

1. Deep, slow breathing. On average, people take between 10 to 14 breaths per minute. See if you can slow this down to six breaths a minute by breathing deeply from your diaphragm, expanding your belly outward on the inhale. Focus on making your exhalations longer and slowing them down substantially. The more you focus on your exhale over your inhale, the more you engage your parasympathetic nervous system.

2. Cold exposure. Dutch athlete Wim Hof has popularized cold exposure as a way to "biohack" your health. Finish your next shower with 30 seconds of very cold water, then increase the amount of time for future showers.

3. Singing, humming, chanting, gargling. Because the vagus nerve and vocal cords and muscles at the back of your throat are connected, practicing the mantram meditation or chakra humming, as described in Chapter 6, can increase vagal tone.

4. Probiotics and omega-3 fatty acids. Research has shown that gut bacteria can improve brain function by affecting the vagus nerve; omega-3 fatty acids, essential fats your body cannot produce on its own, can also increase vagal activity.

5. Meditation. If you can sit in meditation on your own, the energy you produce is beneficial for you and for the world. Not only will you add to a powerful collective energy of mindfulness, but you'll also increase vagal tone and support a feeling of compassion, which is at the heart of many Tibetan Buddhism practices.

TIBETAN DREAM YOGA[86]

Tibetan Bön Lama Tenzin Wangyal Rinpoche (the only Bön master living in the United States) understands that many people in the West have difficulty finding time to practice in their quest for Buddhahood. Yet every human being needs sleep, and we can use this time to understand the deepest aspects of ourselves and help ourselves heal.

Rinpoche's book *The Tibetan Yogas of Dream and Sleep* details how sleep is broken into roughly two-hour segments, and for each working period a particular position is taken, a particular breathing is performed, and the mind focuses on a particular image in a particular chakra.

Given that we sleep a third of our lifetime (that's 20 years for someone who is 60), it's important to be mindful of what happens during dream time. "Every dream is somehow healing, as long as the practitioner is not being distracted by the appearance of the dream and its images and the story of the dream... because you are releasing," Rinpoche observes.

There are four main foundational practices in dream yoga, as outlined by Rinpoche, conducted while awake:

1. Perception. Start your dream practice when you are awake. For everything you see, hear, feel, touch, or smell, say to yourself, "This is a dream." This helps to create nonattachment as you begin to see that everything is transient and a story of perception.

2. Decrease chasing or running away from. When you have a reaction to whatever is happening in your life, the grasping mind may translate this into an emotion such as desire, anger, jealousy, pride, envy, grief, despair, joy, anxiety, depression, fear, boredom... and on and on. When this happens, remind yourself that everything—you, the object, and your reaction—is a dream.

3. Review your day and come back to your intention. As you prepare for sleep, reflect upon your day... then recognize that all of it is a dream. Set a strong intention that during the night when you sleep you will become aware that you are dreaming, so that you can follow this clarity and awareness throughout the night.

4. Find gratitude. When you wake the next day and you realize you've been dreaming, say, "I'm grateful for this." If you haven't had that awareness, don't become discouraged! Instead, focus again on your intention and embark on your awareness practice throughout the day.

Most importantly, release any expectations. Be flexible. Dream yoga is meant to be a joyful, relaxing practice, like taking a warm shower or lying in a comfortable bed.

LIVE IN COMPASSIONATE RELATIONSHIPS

If we were to walk into a room filled with all the people in our lives and then openly and honestly place all our problems on a shared table, we would likely be glad to pull our own problems back. At least once a day, it's helpful to think about the loneliness, confusion, suffering, and ignorance we *all* experience, thereby deepening our sense of compassion.

Everyone is walking a hard path, whether we can see it or not. When we remember this shared human experience, our problems may not seem so serious. We may be able to enjoy life a bit more and even laugh at ourselves, because we understand and appreciate our lives for what they are.

LOVINGKINDNESS METTA MEDITATION

There's a reason that Brené Brown's TED Talk about the power of vulnerability and feeling shame has had more than 54 million views as of this writing. So many of us were taught to hide or run away from our emotions, so we never adequately learned how to express them, how to be bravely courageous, or how to process through our feelings of failure. As Brown asserts, we fall prey to the "belief that if we live perfectly, look perfectly, and act perfectly, we can avoid the pain of blame, judgment, and shame."[87]

Yet perfectionism isn't about growth. Instead, it's about fear and avoidance. Take a moment to visualize all the beings in the world, particularly those who have problems or who are experiencing pain.

Connect with how compassion feels for you, in your body and your being. Begin to imagine sending this energy to all beings on the planet, so that everyone can overcome their obstacles and become healthy and happy. When we have compassion in our hearts and we're able to help a person suffer less, life can take on renewed meaning, leading us to nourishment for the soul and psyche.

When we have compassion in our hearts, and we're able to help a person suffer less, life can take on renewed meaning leading us to nourishment for the soul and psyche.

Let's begin a lovingkindness (metta) practice, inspired by Sylvia Boorstein, founding teacher of Spirit Rock Meditation Center in Woodacre, California:[88]

1. Wherever you are, take a deep breath in, followed by a deep breath out.

2. Begin with a lovingkindness blessing for yourself:

"May I feel safe. May I feel content. May I feel strong. May I live with ease."

3. Bring someone to mind who you love very deeply, someone in your life who's very easy to love, such as a partner, a child, a pet. Focus on just one individual and imagine them before you, saying silently to yourself:

"May you feel safe. May you feel content. May you feel strong. May you live with ease."

4. Bring to mind someone else you love tremendously and repeat:

"May you feel safe. May you feel content. May you feel strong. May you live with ease."

5. Think of someone you may not connect with often, a familiar stranger such as your hair stylist or a barista, and wish for them:

*"May you feel safe. May you feel content. May you feel strong.
May you live with ease."*

6. Says Boorstein, "Think about, past the people that you recognize in the world, familiar strangers, all the unfamiliar strangers, near and far. All around us here and stretching out all around the whole world, all around this whole globe. All people just like us, with lives, who want, just as we do, to live in safety and contentment, to be able to feel strong, to have lives of ease. Who share with us the same wishes and hopes and dreams that we have as human beings. Come home to their family, to be able to take care of their family, celebrate another birthday. Wish this for all of these beings around the planet":

*"May you feel safe. May you feel content. May you feel strong.
May you live with ease."*

7. Before you open your eyes, feel that you are radiating lovingkindness blessings out into the world, wishing for everyone:

*"May you feel safe. May you feel content. May you feel strong.
May you live with ease."*

How does it feel to be in your body, your mind, and your soul now?

THIS IS A HAPPY MOMENT...
IF YOU BELIEVE IT

In his poem "Little Gidding," T. S. Eliot wrote, "We shall not cease from exploration, and the end of all our exploring will be to arrive where we started and know the place for the first time."[89]

We place so much importance on our beliefs because we're sure they are true. Yet a belief is simply a thought that we keep thinking. It's helpful to remember that most disease is caused by stress, and most of our stress comes from a mismatch between our beliefs about life and the life we're actually living. If our beliefs direct our physiology, then perhaps many of our physical and emotional ailments are the result of our bodies being misdirected by ideas that are in conflict with our well-being.

By this logic, when you change your beliefs, you can also change your life. One of the most powerful ways to do this is through mindfulness, reducing the input from the external world, so that you can experience the sense of oneness and inner peace that Tibetan Buddhism describes.

Dr. Andrew Newberg, director of research at the Marcus Institute of Integrative Health in Pennsylvania, found that when Tibetan Buddhists meditate, they exhibit less activity in the brain area that creates a sense of separation between the self and the rest of existence, but more activity in the area that yields a sense of oneness.[90]

Perhaps the truest awakening for our modern lives—especially when we are inundated by social media, consumerism, and a consistent pressure to have more/do more/be more—is the realization that nothing is actually wrong with us. That we don't need "more." In fact, perhaps what we actually need is a lot less—that, as Tibetan Buddhists believe, we are already whole.

We can only be who we already are in each moment. What we call our shadow that we keep wanting to run away from is nothing more simply than an aspect of our nature waiting to be embraced, and reclaimed, to be and loved unconditionally. How would it feel to accept yourself completely?

Cultivating joy takes practice. Many of us think it happens spontaneously, but joy needs to be cultivated, attended to, and practiced. The more you train yourself—the more you explore your own definitions of contentment—the more easily you can find your own harmony.

Buddha described the human mind as being filled with drunken monkeys, jumping around and screeching, chattering, and just carrying on endlessly. You may have heard the term "monkey mind" in yoga or meditation. Every one of us has a monkey mind with dozens of monkeys clamoring for attention. Rather than fighting them, pretending they're not there, or trying to keep them at bay, we can practice the tools and techniques offered throughout this book to create a sense of calm with what is. Meditation can tame the drunken monkeys into loving submission.

Often when we compare ourselves to others, we compare up. We see what it is that others have that we don't. It's rare that we compare ourselves down, seeing who has less than us and perhaps even asking how we could help them. If you can, remind yourself every day how lucky you are, how many conditions of happiness you already have. The fact that your heart is beating, your lungs are breathing. That you can touch and be touched. That you can hug and be held. That when you are doing anything—sitting, walking, driving, eating, talking—you always have an opportunity to breathe in mindfully and breathe out your magical stardust into the world.

Make this present moment a wonderful moment.

"Creation is the transformation of light into matter, and enlightenment is the return of matter back into light. Our physical life's journey begins with the materialization of spirit and ends with the spiritualization of matter. Our consciousness determines what frequencies of the light spectrum we are able to absorb. Those frequencies spiritualize matter into energy, causing us to glow. As consciousness expands, so does our glow. The frequencies of light that we are not yet able to absorb are reflected, attracting back to us matching life experiences that gradually help us embrace what previously disturbed us. When we are able to absorb the entire spectrum of light, 'we' disappear and what remains is a holographic focal point of the sun."

—Joseph Liberman[91]

NOTES

1   Chime Lama, "A Little Fear: Two Poems by Chime Lama," November 26, 2019, Asian American Writers' Workshop, https://aaww.org/two-poems-by-chime-lama.

2   "We're All Made of Stardust. Here's How," *Smithsonian Magazine*, accessed April 1, 2021.

3   Jesse Greenspan, "The Myth of Ponce de León and the Fountain of Youth," HISTORY, A&E Television Networks, last modified April 1, 2020, https://www.history.com/news/the-myth-of-ponce-de-leon-and-the-fountain-of-youth.

4   Peter Kelder, *Ancient Secret of the Fountain of Youth* (New York: Doubleday, 1985), 4.

5   "What Is Buddhist Tantra?," *Tricycle*, accessed July 20, 2021, https://tricycle.org/beginners/buddhism/what-is-buddhist-tantra.

6   Alexander Berzin, "Bon and Tibetan Buddhism," Study Buddhism, Berzin Archives, accessed April 13, 2021, https://studybuddhism.com/en/advanced-studies/abhidharma-tenet-systems/the-tibetan-traditions/bon-and-tibetan-buddhism.

7   "Revisiting the 'Cultural Revolution' in Tibet," The Tibet Museum, accessed April 11, 2021, https://tibetmuseum.org/revisiting-the-cultural-revolution-in-tibet.

8   "Sufism–History," Britannica, accessed April 13, 2021, https://www.britannica.com/topic/Sufism/History.

9   "Learn the 5 Tibetan Rites from Home: Simple, Easy & Affordable," T5T – The Five Tibetans, UnMind Pty Ltd, accessed July 28, 2021, https://t5t.com.

10   John Ira Petty, "China's Wall Less Great from Space," NASA, May 9, 2005, https://www.nasa.gov/vision/space/workinginspace/great _wall.html.

11   Ann Gibbons, "Tibetans Inherited High-Altitude Gene from Ancient Human," *Science*, American Association for the Advancement of Science, July 2, 2014, https://www.sciencemag.org/news/2014/07/ tibetans-inherited-high-altitude-gene-ancient-human#:~:text= Researchers%20discovered%20in%202010%20that,the%20body's% 20production%20of%20hemoglobin.

12   Barbara Demick, *Eat the Buddha: Life and Death in a Tibetan Town* (New York: Random House, 2020), xiv.

13   Demick, *Eat the Buddha*, 16.

14   "Buddha Eyes—Wisdom Eyes, Meaning, Buddhist Symbols & Images," Source Nepal, accessed March 18, 2021, https://www.source nepal.com/buddha-eye-meaning/#:~:text=In%20stupas%2C%20 there%20are%20giant,we%20can%20fulfill%20our%20dreams.

15   "Buddha Eyes—Wisdom Eyes," 22.

16   "Tibet – Tibet since 1900," Brittanica, accessed April 1, 2021, https://www.britannica.com/place/Tibet/Tibet-since-1900.

17   "Tibetan Astrology," Nangten Menlang International, accessed March 24, 2021, https://tulkulobsang.org/en/tibetan-knowledge/ tibetan-astrology.

18   Kajsa Landgren, "Pulse Diagnosis," ScienceDirect, 2008, https:// www.sciencedirect.com/topics/medicine-and-dentistry/pulse- diagnosis.

19   Evan Osnos, "The Next Incarnation," *The New Yorker*, September 27, 2010, https://www.newyorker.com/magazine/2010/10/04/the-next-incarnation.

20   His Holiness the XIV Dalai Lama, *The Path to Bliss: A Practical Guide to the Stages of Meditation* (Snow Lion, 1991), https://tibethouse.us/tibetan-calendar-astrological-diagram.

21   Chögyal Namkhai Norbu and Fabio Andrico, *Tibetan Yoga of Movement: The Art and Practice of Yantra Yoga* (Berkeley, CA: North Atlantic Books, 2003), xiv–xvi.

22   "Tibetan Medicine," Nangten Menlang International, accessed March 24, 2021, https://tulkulobsang.org/en/tibetan-knowledge/tibetan-medicine.

23   Chime Lama, "A Little Fear: Two Poems by Chime Lama."

24   Norbu and Andrico, *Tibetan Yoga of Movement*, xiii.

25   Elaine Lipson, "Unraveling the Mystery of Tibetan Yoga Practices," *Yoga Journal*, August 29, 2007, https://www.yogajournal.com/yoga-101/mystic.

26   Norbu and Andrico, *Tibetan Yoga of Movement*, xiii.

27   "Questions and Answers," Dzogchen Center, accessed July 23, 2021, https://dzogchen.org/resources/questions-answers.

28   "[Video download] Eight Movements," Shang Shung Publications, accessed July 23, 2021, https://shop.shangshungfoundation.com/en/products/2000000008790_video-download-eight-movements-gliotto-movimenti-yantra-yoga-mp4.html.

29   Elaine Lipson, "Unraveling the Mystery of Tibetan Yoga Practices," *Yoga Journal*, August 29, 2007, https://www.yogajournal.com/yoga-101/mystic.

30   Norbu and Andrico, *Tibetan Yoga of Movement*, xiv–xv.

31 Peter Kelder, *The Eye of Revelation* (Bradenton, FL: Booklocker. com, Inc., 2008), 81.

32 Gretchen Stelter, "Chakras: A Beginner's Guide to the 7 Chakras," Healthline, last modified December 18, 2016, healthline.com/health/ fitness-exercise/7-chakras.

33 Christopher S. Kilham, *The Five Tibetans* (Rochester, VT: Healing Arts Press, 1994), 15–25.

34 Kathryn Budig, *The Women's Health Big Book of Yoga* (New York: Rodale, 2012), 298–299.

35 "Wim Hof Method Breathing," Wim Hof Method, accessed April 8, 2021, https://www.wimhofmethod.com/breathing-exercises.

36 Emily Cronkleton, "What Is Breathwork?," Healthline, December 3, 2018, https://www.healthline.com/health/breathwork.

37 Adrienne A. Taren et al., "Mindfulness Meditation Training Alters Stress-Related Amygdala Resting State Functional Connectivity: A Randomized Controlled Trial," *Social Cognitive and Affective Neuroscience* 10, no. 12, December 2015, https://doi.org/10.1093/ scan/nsv066.

38 Helen Lavretsky and Paul A. Newhouse, "Stress, Inflammation and Aging," *American Journal of Geriatric Psychiatry: Official Journal of the American Association for Geriatric Psychiatry, 20*(9), September 1, 2013, https://doi.org/10.1097/JGP.0b013e31826573cf.

39 Kilham, *The Five Tibetans*, 32–36.

40 Tenzing Rigdol, "Anthology of Tibetan Poets," Big Bridge, accessed March 13, 2021, https://bigbridge.org/BB17/poetry/ anthologyoftibetanpoets/Tenzing_Rigdol.html.

41 Brené Brown, "Brené with Emily and Amelia Nagoski on Burnout and How to Complete the Stress Cycle," October 14, 2020, in *Unlocking Us*, produced by Cadence 13, podcast, MP3 audio, https://brenebrown.com/podcast/brene-with-emily-and-amelia-nagoski-on-burnout-and-how-to-complete-the-stress-cycle/#close-popup.

42 Kelder, *The Eye of Revelation*, 85–91.

43 Kelder, *Ancient Secret of the Fountain of Youth*, 32–39.

44 Cara Tabachnick, "Here's What You Should Know before Attending a Whirling Dervish Ceremony in Turkey," *Washington Post*, April 12, 2019, https://www.washingtonpost.com/lifestyle/travel/heres-what-you-should-know-before-attending-a-whirling-dervish-ceremony-in-turkey/2019/04/11/1af4bbac-57af-11e9-9136-f8e636f1f6df_story.html, April 12, 2019.

45 Kelder, *Ancient Secret of the Fountain of Youth*, 48–54.

46 Kelder, *Ancient Secret of the Fountain of Youth*, 53.

47 Khawa Nyingchak, "Farewell Words," High Peaks Pure Earth, June 26, 2016, https://highpeakspureearth.com/farewell-words-by-and-for-khawa-nyingchak.

48 Demick, *Eat the Buddha*, 14–16.

49 "China Urged to Release Panchen Lama after 20 Years," BBC, May 17, 2015, https://www.bbc.com/news/world-asia-china-32771242.

50 "Library of Tibetan Works & Archives," accessed April 17, 2021, https://tibetanlibrary.org.

51 Ngodup Paljor, "Anthology of Tibetan Poets," Big Bridge, accessed April 17, 2021, https://bigbridge.org/BB17/poetry/anthology oftibetanpoets/Ngodup_Paljor.html#.

52 John Powers, *Introduction to Tibetan Buddhism* (Ithaca, NY: Snow Lion Publications, 1995), https://www.pbs.org/wgbh/pages/frontline/shows/tibet/understand/bon.html.

53 Anastasiia Ilina, "11 Beautiful Words That Will Make You Fall in Love With the Tibetan Language," Culture Trip, July 10, 2019, https://theculturetrip.com/asia/articles/12-words-that-will-make-you-fall-in-love-with-the-tibetan-language.

54 Principal Commitments," His Holiness The 14th Dalai Lama of Tibet, accessed February 1, 2021, https://www.dalailama.com/the-dalai-lama/biography-and-daily-life/three-main-commitments.

55 John Ambenge, *Sociology* (PA: Page Publishing, 2020).

56 "Six Realms of Rebirth," Oxford Reference, accessed March 3, 2021, https://www.oxfordreference.com/view/10.1093/oi/authority.20110803100509423.

57 Tarthang Tulku, *Gesture of Balance* (Berkeley, CA: Dharma Publishing, 1977), ix–x.

58 "What Are the Three Jewels?," *Lion's Roar*, May 9, 2017, https://www.lionsroar.com/what-are-the-three-jewels.

59 Tarthang Tulku, *Gesture of Balance* (Berkeley, CA: Dharma Publishing, 1977).

60 History.com Editors, "Buddhism," last modified July 22, 2020, https://www.history.com/topics/religion/buddhism, HISTORY, A&E Television Networks.

61 Jacob Israel Liberman, *Luminous Life: How the Science of Light Unlocks the Art of Living* (Novato, CA: New World Library, 2018), 15.

62 Glen Swartwout, "Dark Energy Is Condensed Light in New Theory," Newswire Network Ltd, May 23, 2014, https://newswire.net/newsroom/pr/00082623-dark-energy.html.

63   World of Work Project, accessed July 28, 2021, https://world ofwork.io/2019/07/who-am-i.

64   Tulku, *Gesture of Balance*, ix–x.

65   Tulku, *Gesture of Balance*, 26.

66   "Our Three Brains — The Reptilian Brain," Interaction Design Foundation, accessed July 28, 2021, https://www.interaction-design. org/literature/article/our-three-brains-the-reptilian-brain.

67   Kain Ramsey, "The Three Levels of Human Consciousness," Medium, March 7, 2019, https://medium.com/achology/the-three-levels-of-human-consciousness-6d9a59fed577.

68   Ezequiel Morsella et al., "Homing in on Consciousness in the Nervous System: An Action-Based Synthesis." *Behavioral and Brain Sciences* 39 (2016): E168. https://doi.org/doi:10.1017/S0140525 X15000643.

69   Liberman, *Luminous Life*, 68.

70   Liberman, *Luminous Life*, 120.

71   "Joe Dispenza on How to Reprogram Your Subconscious Mind," Fearless Motivation, November 7, 2019, https://www.fearless motivation.com/2019/11/07/joe-dispenza-on-how-to-reprogram-your-subconscious-mind.

72   Kelder, *Ancient Secret of the Fountain of Youth*, 79–93.

73   Liberman, *Luminous Life*, 91.

74   Liberman, *Luminous Life*, 70.

75   Rollo May, "Foreward," in *Existential-Phenomenological Alternatives for Psychology*, eds. Ronald S. Valle and Mark King, (NY: Oxford University Press, June 1, 1978).

76   Marianne Schnall, "Exclusive Interview with Zen Master Thich Nhat Hanh," HuffPost, Buzzfeed Inc., last modified December 6, 2017, https://www.huffpost.com/entry/beliefs-buddhism-exclusiv_b_577541.

77   Ethan Siegal, "You Are Not Mostly Empty Space," *Forbes*, April 16, 2020, https://www.forbes.com/sites/startswithabang/2020/04/16/you-are-not-mostly-empty-space/?sh=4fa9ef02c2b0.

78   "20 Amazing Things About the Human Body," Martha Stewart, Meredith Corporation, February 13, 2011, https://www.martha stewart.com/267590/20-amazing-things-about-the-human-body.

79   Based on the teachings of artist and scientist Rudolf Steiner, Waldorf schools take a holistic approach to education that integrates arts and practical skills with academics.

80   Kelder, *Ancient Secret of the Fountain of Youth*, 75.

81   "Stress Effects on the Body," American Psychological Association, November 1, 2018, https://www.apa.org/topics/stress/body.

82   "Jon Kabat-Zinn Professional Background – Mindfulness Meditations," Mindfulnesscds.com, accessed July 28, 2021, https://www.mindfulnesscds.com/pages/about-the-author.

83   For detailed information, see Vibha Kumar, "Stress, the Root of Most Illnesses: Research," *Hindustan Times*, last modified June 3, 2014, https://www.hindustantimes.com/health-and-fitness/stress-the-root-of-most-illnesses-research/story-4VOG9pWDbzSO4QdiYR2r ZN.html.

84   Jordan Rosenfeld, "9 Fascinating Facts about the Vagus Nerve," *Mental Floss*, November 13, 2018, https://www.mentalfloss.com/article/65710/9-nervy-facts-about-vagus-nerve.

85   Jordan Fallis, "How to Stimulate Your Vagus Nerve for Better Mental Health," September 2, 2021, https://www.optimal livingdynamics.com/blog/how-to-stimulate-your-vagus-nerve-for-better-mental-health-brain-vns-ways-treatment-activate-natural-foods-depression-anxiety-stress-heart-rate-variability-yoga-massage-vagal-tone-dysfunction.

86   Tenzin Wangyal Rinpoche, "The Tibetan Yogas of Dream and Sleep," Shambhala Publications, accessed April 14, 2021, https://www.shambhala.com/snowlion_articles/the-tibetan-yogas-of-dream-and-sleep.

87   Matt Valentine, "5 Life-Altering Lessons from Brené Brown's The Power of Vulnerability," Goalcast, June 18, 2018, https://www.goalcast.com/2018/06/18/5-lessons-brene-brown-the-power-of-vulnerability.

88   Sylvia Boorstein, "A Lovingkindness Meditation," On Being Project, May 8, 2017, https://onbeing.org/blog/sylvia-boorstein-a-lovingkindness-meditation.

89   T. S. Eliot, "Little Gidding," Columbia University, accessed July 18, 2021, http://www.columbia.edu/itc/history/winter/w3206/edit/tseliotlittlegidding.html.

90   Andrew Newberg, "Research Questions—Andy Newberg," Andy Newberg, accessed July 28, 2021, http://www.andrewnewberg.com/research.

91   Liberman, *Luminous Life*, 140.

ACKNOWLEDGMENTS

Thank you to my incredible daughter. Always and forever, you have shown me how to love more wildly. Thank you also to my amazing surf mamas and papas community. You all are the reason I can be who I would like to be.

ABOUT THE AUTHOR

Judy Tsuei is a holistic practitioner and the founder of Wild Hearted Words, a strategic content marketing agency where she creates health, wellness, and mindfulness content for renowned global brands. An advocate for mental and emotional health for Asian Americans, she also hosts the F*ck Saving Face podcast, a show that breaks through taboo topics within the Asian Americans and Pacific Islanders community. She currently lives in San Diego, California, with her daughter, Wilder Love. Stay in touch at www.wildheartedwords.com and www.fcksavingface.com.